D0185825

weber's
ultimate
barbecue
book

weber's
ultimate
barbecue
book

matthew drennan

photography chris alack

MQ
MQ Publications Ltd

Published by MQ Publications Ltd.
Unit 12, The Ivories, 6–8 Northampton Street,
London N1 2HY

Copyright © Weber-Stephen Products Co. 2001
Illustrations © Marc Dando 2001

All rights reserved. No part of this publication may be reproduced
or transmitted in any form or by any means, electronic or
mechanical, including photocopy, recording, or any information
storage and retrieval system now known or to be invented
without permission in writing from the publisher.

Editorial Team:

    Managing Editor: Ljiljana Ortolja-Baird
    Editors: Kate John, Marian Temesvary
    Photography: Chris Alack
    Food styling: Carol Tennant, Matthew Drennan
    Illustrations: Marc Dando
    Cover design: Simon Balley
    Book design concept: Broadbase
    Page layout: Yvonne Dedman
    Recipe credits: Matthew Drennan; Sunset Books Inc;
      Weber-Stephen Products Company.
    Photographic credits: Weber-Stephen Products Co;
    Stephen Hamilton, p10 (bottom left), p23, p145

Produced by:

    MQ Publications Ltd under exclusive licence from
    Weber-Stephen Products Co.

    MQ Publications:
      Zaro Weil, CEO & Publisher
    Weber-Stephen Products Co:
      Mike Kempster, Sr, Executive Vice President;
      Marian Temesvary, Director of Marketing.

Heatbeads® is a registered trademark of Australian Char Pty Ltd.

A CIP catalogue record for this book is available
from the British Library

ISBN: 1 84072 265 7

Printed and bound in Great Britain by Butler & Tanner Ltd, Frome
and London.

3 5 7 9 8 6 4 2

contents

foreword

At Weber, we have a long and happy tradition of barbecuing. Since George Stephen invented the Weber kettle grill in 1952, we have made grilling our business. Over the next 25 years, we turned what originally looked like a strange object that people called a 'Sputnik' into an icon of the American lifestyle. Then in 1985 we once again revolutionized outdoor barbecuing by introducing the 'Genesis' series of gas grills which have also become a beloved feature of the backyard scene.

Recognising that barbecuing is an ancient form of cooking indigenous to many cultures, we decided to explore the world beyond our borders and bring our products and grilling enthusiasm to other countries. So in 1976, I flew to Cologne to attend our first European trade exhibit. I knew nothing about European grilling habits or cultural differences, but figured that if we could just get people to see and use our kettle barbecues they would be converted to the 'Weber way'. The reaction to our products was very encouraging and since then we have built a loyal following of grilling enthusiasts throughout Europe. Indeed, it has been a great learning experience over the years. We have talked to consumers at demonstrations and listened to their barbecuing stories, both the successes and horrors. We have tried many local recipes and foods, adapting them to our products with wonderful results.

Hence this cookbook. We wanted to feature recipes and foods that celebrate the broad spectrum of flavours and ingredients that European and other world cuisines have brought to barbecued food. This book uniquely showcases the meats, fish, fowl and local dishes of European countries. The recipes were created by our team of European food specialists – an award-winning chef, writer, photographer and publisher – and carefully tested by locals. They include both the traditional, as well as more exotic, cuisines that European cooking has heartily embraced, for example, Asian and African spices and flavours. Each recipe combines foolproof grilling methods and fresh ingredients, thereby accentuating the characteristic flavours of the food.

Every occasion and appetite has been carefully catered to, thanks to the vast array of recipes featured.

The book celebrates different courses with equal relish, giving you the option to prepare – amongst other meals – a sumptuous four-course banquet, an intimate supper, or an easy family lunch.

During the development of this book I have had a chance to sift through the recipes and try them out on my own grill in Chicago. The diversity of recipes reminds me of the many delicious barbecues I have enjoyed with my European friends.

Incorporating familiar as well as inspirational recipes, I hope the book will tempt your tastebuds and encourage you to use your barbecue as often as possible. Any recipe you select, any tip you learn and apply, will help you create a memorable outdoor meal with family and friends.

Enjoy and Bon Appetit!

Mike Kempster

Mike Kempster, Sr.
Executive Vice President
Weber-Stephen Products Co.

introduction

Barbecuing or outdoor grilling is an essential part of modern living. For many years 'getting out the barbecue' has been a favourite event across the nation, bringing people together to relax, cook and enjoy the good life *al fresco*. Who, after all, can resist the distinctive flavours and tempting aromas of succulent grilled fish, meat, or vegetables on a warm summer evening?

We used to think of barbecuing as cooking basic fare for a crowd – hamburgers, sausages, the occasional steak or chop. But over the years we've incorporated many other culinary traditions into our grilling repertoire, introducing a long list of new ingredients as well as a tasty twist on the more familiar foods. In this book we started with the basics, keeping things simple and focusing on those ingredients that are readily available in your local supermarket.

The trick to successful barbecuing is using the right equipment. We believe that means a barbecue with a lid. (The best barbecue 'kettles' have fitted lids, while most gas barbecues have either an attached or removable lid.) When food is cooked over an open fire, not only does it take longer to cook, but many of the wonderful juices and flavours either evaporate or are singed out of the food. A lid keeps the food moist, allows the heat to circulate, and generally cuts down on cooking time. It also flavours the food with that fantastic smoky taste that can even be achieved on a gas barbecue. You could say that grilling without a lid is a bit like trying to bake a cake with the oven door still open!

Many enthusiasts wonder which kind of barbecue is best: gas or charcoal? Blind taste tests have shown that most people can't tell the difference between one or the other, and both types have their benefits. Some prefer the more traditional hands-on activity of building and starting the fire with a charcoal grill, while others prefer the quick, clean convenience of a gas grill. Rest assured that whichever you choose, you are on the right road to successful grilling with this book. All of the recipes have been created and tested using gas and charcoal barbecues, and each recipe gives precise directions for both types. Charcoal and gas barbecues are ideal for grilling by either the Direct or Indirect method, on which the recipes in this book are based. Direct grilling simply means putting the food directly over the heat source; while in Indirect grilling the food is placed between the sources of heat, which rotate inside the barbecue, much like a convection oven.

In Barbecue Basics, we show you how to set up your grill – whether you use gas or charcoal; how to light and control the fire with confidence; how to keep the barbecue grill clean; and how to achieve smoking techniques with the right materials. Each chapter gives an introduction to perfecting the basics: searing steaks, keeping a chicken breast moist, perfecting the art of grill marks on food, achieving succulent fish fillets that don't stick to the grill, and many other techniques that will help you build your barbecuing expertise. 'Cook's tips' are scattered throughout the recipes to clarify certain methods, and there is even a discussion about the best tools to use for successful outdoor grilling.

All that being said, the real key to successful barbecuing is to have fun! Keeping the ingredients and menu simple, planning the various steps, and sharing the experience with family and friends are sure-fire ways to enjoy good food and a good time. This book is a celebration of outdoor cooking with a choice of recipes to make the occasion as simple or spectacular as you like. We've included all the basics you'll need, plus some recipes to inspire you to stretch your repertoire. So, come rain or shine, great outdoor grilling starts here . . .

Key to recipes

Recipe Guideline	Degree of Difficulty
✳	Simple
✳ ✳	Moderate
✳ ✳ ✳	Advanced

barbecue basics

This chapter introduces you to the ease of setting up, lighting and using your charcoal or gas barbecue, including what kind of fuel to use and how to get a great smokey flavour. It describes both the Direct and Indirect cooking methods, giving you flexibility in barbecuing. You can learn how to use your grill to suit the food you are planning to cook, from a simple chicken breast to a leg of lamb. Cooking and safety guidelines are provided, as well as advice on barbecue accessories, and tips on how to keep barbecuing simple and fun.

Many of the recipes in the book use delicious marinades, rubs and flavored butters to enhance the food and lock in flavor. Tried and tested recipes for these are featured in this chapter, most of which can be made in advance.

In short, this chapter is aimed at making your barbecue experience as easy, safe and successful as possible. So let's get started!

charcoal grills

The secret of cooking on a charcoal kettle lies in the proper use of the lid and the air damper system, along with two proven methods of positioning the charcoal briquettes. Cold air is drawn through the bottom vents to provide the oxygen necessary to keep the coals burning. The air heats and rises and is reflected off the lid, so it circulates around the food being cooked, eventually passing out through the top vent. Thus a kettle grill cooks in the same manner as a convection oven, making it ideal for roasts and whole poultry, in addition to the more common steaks and sausages.

Remember the temperature is always higher at the start of cooking and as the coals burn down the temperature will gradually fall. For Indirect cooking, adding coals every hour to each side will maintain a consistent grilling temperature (see chart on page 17 for quantities).

How to light your charcoal grill

1 Remove the lid and open all air vents before building the fire.

2 Spread the charcoal over the charcoal grate (the heavy grate at the bottom of the kettle), then pile it into a mound in the centre. Spreading the charcoal over the grate first helps you determine how much you need.

3 Insert 4 or 5 firelighters (see **figure 1**).

4 Light the firelighters and let the coals catch and burn (see **figure 2**) until they are covered with a light grey ash. This usually takes about 25-30 minutes. You can also use a chimney starter (see note on page 13). Then, using tongs arrange the coals according to the cooking method you are going to use, the Direct or Indirect method. Finally, place the cooking grate over the coals. The grill is now ready (see **figure 3**).

figure 1   figure 2   figure 3

Lighting agents

■ **Firelighters** Barbecue firelighters are waxy-looking cubes or sticks, which are designed to light the barbecue without giving off any harmful fumes that could taint the food. Push four or five into the charcoal and light with a taper or a long stem match. They are easy to use, clean and safe. (Only use firelighters designed for barbecues.) Do not use firelighters designed for domestic fires as they contain paraffin, which will spoil the food.

■ **Firelighter fluid** If using this product handle with care. It should be sprayed on the dry coals, left for a few minutes to soak in, then ignited with a taper or long stem match. Never spray on hot or burning coals because the flames can travel up into the bottle causing serious burns.

Chimney starter

A metal canister with a handle, a chimney starter holds a supply of charcoal. Crumpled newspaper or firelighters are put on the cooking grate and lit, the chimney starter filled with coals and positioned over the firelighters. The walls of the chimney starter focus the flames and heat onto the charcoal, thereby decreasing the amount of time it takes for the coals to light and ash over. Once the coals are ready, simply tip the coals onto the grate and arrange them for grilling as shown in **figures 5 and 8**.

Direct cooking

This method of grilling is recommended for steaks, chops, kebabs, sausages, vegetables and foods that take less than 25 minutes to cook through. Remember to always cook with the lid on for best results.

1 Prepare and light the charcoal grill as demonstrated on page 12, then spread the coals in an even layer across the charcoal grate (see **figure 5**).

2 Place the food on the cooking grate, cover with the lid and cook directly over the heat source (see **figure 6**). The heat cooks the food from directly underneath (see **figure 4**). The food should be turned once halfway through the recommended grilling time.

Direct cooking

figure 4

figure 5

figure 6

Indirect cooking

This method is recommended for roasts, ribs, whole poultry and other large cuts of meat which take longer than 25 minutes. For best results always cook with the lid on.

1 Prepare and light the charcoal grill as demonstrated on page 12 and then arrange the coals evenly on each side of the charcoal grate using charcoal rails or baskets to stabilize. Place a foil drip pan in the centre of the grate between the burning coals (see **figure 8**). This prevents flare-ups particularly when cooking fatty foods and it's useful for collecting drippings, for gravies and sauces.

2 Place the food in the centre of the cooking grate, then cover with the lid and cook Indirectly (see **figure 9**). The heat rises around the food, reflecting off the inside surfaces of the kettle, and cooks the food evenly on all sides (see **figure 7**). This circulating heat works like a convection oven, so there is no need to turn the food. Charcoal briquettes will need to be added each hour to maintain a constant roasting temperature (see chart on page 17).

Indirect cooking

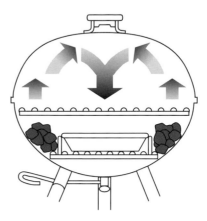

figure 7

figure 8

figure 9

Smoking on a charcoal grill

You can add a more distinctive flavour to barbecued foods by adding natural or manufactured flavourings to the smouldering coals before cooking. Soaking any materials used in smoking helps to create the smoke flavour and aroma. There are many flavoured wood chips available on the market today, such as apple, cherry, maple, hickory, oak, and pecan. These should be soaked in cold water for about 30 minutes prior to adding to the coals. Natural flavours include woody stalks of herbs such as rosemary, bay or thyme, and even grapevines. Simply lay the wet stalks on the coals before you begin cooking the food. You can also use walnut, almond or hazelnut shells that should be soaked for about 30 minutes before using.

Charcoal Fuel

There are many different brands of charcoal but there are only two main types, charcoal briquettes and lumpwood. Lumpwood burns hotter and faster than briquettes.

■ **Charcoal briquettes** These are even sized lumps of fuel made from particles of charcoal mixed with a starch binder. They tend to burn longer than lumpwood charcoal. There are two types of briquettes – the larger, traditional squarish ones, and smaller round ones also known as Heatbeads®. These burn somewhat faster than traditional briquettes – consult the chart opposite for comparisons. It is a good idea to count the briquettes you use. After a while, you will become familiar with the quantity required and you will be able to judge it visually. Use the chart opposite to determine how many briquettes you require, depending on the type used.

■ **Lumpwood charcoal** This is not fossilized fuel extracted from the ground like coal, but is in fact wood that has been fired in a kiln. The process burns the wood without setting fire to it and drives out all the by-products, leaving behind a very light black combustible form of carbon. Opt for good quality brands, which give you larger pieces that light easier and burn better and are less likely to fall through the charcoal grate as they burn down. Instant lighting lumpwood charcoal is also available, which has been impregnated with a lighting agent and comes in a sealed paper bag. The whole bag is placed in the barbecue and ignited.

Because this type of charcoal requires wood from trees for its manufacture, unregulated deforestation became a concern as the world-wide popularity of barbecuing increased. There is now an international organisation called the Forest Stewardship Council (FSC) sponsored by the World Wildlife Fund that monitors and regulates the use of trees from selected areas of forest. Look for charcoal with the FSC logo.

Woody herbs such as rosemary can be scattered on the hot coals just before cooking to add flavour to the food.

How many briquettes you need to use

BBQ Kettle	Square Traditional briquettes	Round Charcoal beads
37cm (14½ in) diameter	8–16 each side	12–24 each side
47cm (18½ in) diameter	16–32 each side	28–56 each side
57cm (22½ in) diameter	25–50 each side	44–88 each side
95cm (37½ in) diameter	4–8kg each side	4–8kg each side
Charcoal Go-Anywhere®	8–16 each side	12–24 each side

How many briquettes you need to add per hour for Indirect cooking

BBQ Kettle	Number of coals per side / per hour
37cm (14½ in) diameter	6
47cm (18½ in) diameter	7
57cm (22½ in) diameter	9
95cm (37½ in) diameter	22
Charcoal Go-Anywhere®	6

gas grills

Gas grills have one main advantage over charcoal and that's speed. Once your gas bottle is attached it's as simple as turning on the convection oven in your kitchen. Simply flick the ignition switch and within about ten to fifteen minutes the barbecue is up to heat and ready to use.

Gas barbecues are run on Liquid Petroleum (LP) gas which comes in two forms, butane or propane. The gas is under moderate pressure in the cylinder and is liquid. As the pressure is released the liquid vaporizes and becomes a gas.

How to light your gas grill

1 Check there is enough fuel in your tank (some grills have gauges to measure how much gas is in the tank). Check to see all the burner control knobs are turned off. Open the lid.

2 Turn the gas valve on the bottle to 'on'.

3 Turn on one burner and light the grill according to the manufacturer's directions using either the ignition switch or a match. When the gas flame has ignited, turn on the other burners.

4 Close the lid and preheat the grill until the thermometer reads 500–550°F, 245–275°C. This takes about 10–15 minutes. Then adjust the burner controls according to the cooking method, Direct (see **figure 10**) or Indirect (see **figure 12**), you are going to use. The grill is now ready for cooking.

■ **Always read the safety instructions carefully on transporting, storing and fitting gas bottles.**

Smoking on a gas grill

It's easy to smoke food on a gas grill. Soak your choice of wood chips in cold water for 30 minutes (see discussion on the various smoking materials on page 16). Put into a small foil pan or a smoker box accessory. (If using a foil pan, remove the cooking grate, place the foil pan in the front left hand corner of the grill directly on top of the heat source, and then replace the cooking grate.) Ignite and preheat the grill. Smoke will form during the preheating stage before the food goes on the grill. Once the grill is up to heat and smoke has formed, place the food in the centre of the cooking grate and grill according to the recipe. Never place food directly over the pan of smoking wood chips.

Cleaning your grill

The easiest way to keep your grill clean is to heat it up and clean it before cooking, each time. When the barbecue is hot, use a long-handled grill brush or crumpled aluminium foil to rub the loosened particles from the cooking grates. The heat virtually 'sterilises' the cooking grates, and brushing them eliminates any remnant flavours, fats or food particles. This cleaning tip applies equally to charcoal grills.

Left: **A smoker box accessory makes adding smokey flavour on your gas grill easy and convenient.**

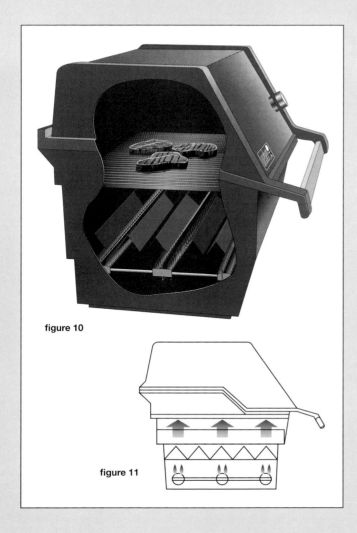

figure 10

figure 11

Indirect cooking

This method is recommended for roasts, ribs, whole poultry and other large cuts of meat which take longer than 25 minutes. For best results always cook with the lid on.

Ignite the grill, and turn all burners onto High, close lid and leave to come up to heat. Place the food in the centre of the cooking grate and turn off the burner(s) directly below the food. Adjust the burners on either side of the food to the temperature according to the recipe. Close the lid and cook Indirectly (see **figure 12**). The heat rises around the food and reflects off the inside surfaces of the grill cooking the food evenly on all sides. This circulating heat works like a convection oven, so there's no need to turn the food (see **figure 13**).

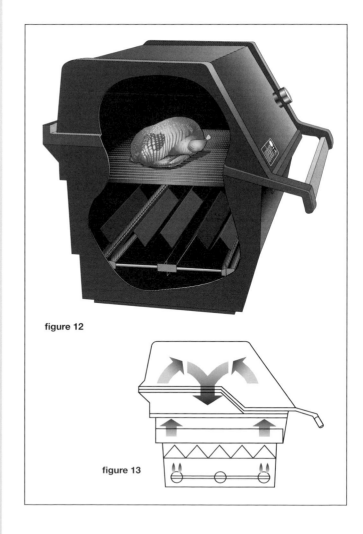

figure 12

figure 13

Direct cooking

This method of grilling is recommended for steaks, chops, kebabs, sausages, vegetables and foods that take less than 25 minutes to cook through. Remember to always cook with the lid on for best results.

Ignite the grill, and turn all burners onto High, close the lid and leave to come up to heat. Adjust the burners to the required temperature according to your recipe. Place the food on the cooking grate (see **figure 10**). Close the lid and cook Directly over the heat source. The heat cooks the food from directly underneath (see **figure 11**). The food should be turned once halfway through the cooking time.

helpful grilling tips & hints

Cooking guidelines

- Make sure charcoal and gas grills are up to temperature before cooking.

- Always cook with the lid down for best results.

- Grilling times in charts and recipes are approximate because times vary depending on the amount, size and shape of food and the weather. Allow a little more cooking time on colder days and less cooking time in extremely hot weather.

- A crowded cooking grate of food will require a little more cooking time than a few pieces of food. Make sure that individual pieces of food do not touch, allowing the heat to cook all sides.

- Trim excess fat from steaks, chops and roasts leaving no more than a 5mm/¼ inch thick layer. This helps avoid flare-ups.

- When using a marinade, glaze or sauce with a high sugar content, or any other ingredient that burns easily, only brush on the food during the last 10–15 minutes of cooking.

- Spatulas or tongs are best for turning food on the grill, but avoid flattening foods such as burgers, which results in juices and flavours escaping.

Safety guidelines

- **Stand the barbecue or grill in a sheltered place, on a firm level surface away from buildings and anything else that could catch fire such as fences and trees.**

- **Never try and start a barbecue when it's very windy.**

- **Always carefully follow the manufacturers' specific instructions as to proper use.**

- **Keep children and pets away from the heat source and potentially hot utensils.**

- **Leave perishable foods in the fridge or a cool box until just before cooking.**

- **Remember to use separate utensils such as chopping boards and plates for raw and cooked foods.**

- **Make sure sausages and poultry are thoroughly cooked through before removing from the grill.**

- **Always use long-handled tools, and cover your hand with an oven mitt to avoid burns.**

- **Stainless steel skewers will retain a lot of heat for a time after being removed from the grill. Make sure you remind your guests.**

- **Be sure to chill any leftover cooked food from the grill once it has cooled.**

- **Check hot coals are fully extinguished before leaving the barbecue site.**

- **Remember the golden rule 'water and fire do not mix'. Some people believe keeping a water bottle or spray at hand is useful to douse flare-ups. This is not true. Steam vapours can cause serious burns and cold water sprayed on a hot grill can damage the porcelain–enamel finish of the grill. To prevent flare-ups occurring in the first place, make sure excess fat is trimmed from poultry and meats. If flare-ups do occur, move the food to one side until the flames have subsided.**

Trouble shooting guidelines

Most outdoor cooks find their own path to success through trial and error but watch out for these common pitfalls.

- **Be patient when lighting a charcoal grill.** It takes a good 25-30 minutes to reach the desired temperature. This is indicated when a light grey ash covers the coals. Putting the food on before the coals are ready can actually lengthen the cooking time, and even toughen meat, affecting the flavour. Also, flavour can be affected by fluid or firelighters that may not have burnt out properly.

- **Do not be over zealous using combustible lighter fluid,** which can lead to serious fires. Never use petrol or other highly volatile fluid to ignite charcoal. Only use a commercially prepared lighter fluid, and allow it to soak-in before igniting. Never add firelighter fluid to hot or warm charcoal. Always follow manufacturer's instructions on all fire starters and use sparingly.

- **Different foods require different cooking methods** so be sure to choose the right one. It is important to understand the difference between Direct and Indirect cooking.

- **Avoid frequent peeking at the food.** Every time the lid is lifted, heat escapes, increasing the cooking time . Calculate the cooking time and only open the lid to add coals (for charcoal grills), basting or turning foods.

- **Do not close the air vents at the top or the bottom on a charcoal grill during cooking** because they help air circulate and keep the coals burning when open.

- **Avoid turning the food too frequently.** In most cases and primarily when using the Direct method, turning the food once halfway through the calculated cooking time is sufficient.

- **Avoid using a fork to pierce and turn small cuts of meat** as this creates holes that allow the juices and flavour to flow out, leaving the meat dry.

- **Many people think that grilling meat for a short time at a high temperature seals in the juices.** This will, however, burn the meat on the outside while leaving it still raw in the centre. It's better to 'sear' meat for a few minutes over Direct heat and move it to Indirect heat for the remainder of the grilling time for best results.

- **Never line the bottom of a grill or cover the cooking grate with tin foil.** This obstructs the airflow in the grill. Covering the grate can also result in puddles of grease accumulating which can lead to flare-ups.

accessories

While there's no need to buy every gadget ever invented for outdoor cooking, there are a few essentials that will make the job easier and, more importantly, safer. A general rule of thumb is to choose long handled tools.

■ An extra wide metal **spatula** is best for turning burgers, steaks and delicate fish fillets. A good sturdy stainless steel blade is best.

■ A **basting brush** is a must for brushing the food or cooking grate lightly with oil before cooking, to prevent food from sticking. This can also be used to brush food during cooking. Choose one with natural bristles.

■ A brass bristle **grill brush** makes cleaning the cooking grate easier. When the grill is hot, brush off food residue. Brass is rust resistant, so it's best for outdoors.

■ A pair of spring-hinged **tongs** is great for lifting and turning most types of food. Choose one with stainless steel ends and long handles.

■ A **long handled fork** helps lift cooked roasts and whole poultry from the grill. Avoid piercing food while it's cooking because valuable juices will be lost. Also avoid using a fork on smaller cuts of meat.

■ A good quality **oven glove** provides protection from pans or utensils and the grill itself. A gauntlet style glove also helps protect the cook's forearm.

■ A **timer** is not essential but is a very useful accessory for one reason in particular: cooking under a lid puts the food out of sight and sometimes out of mind, especially if you are nipping in and out to the kitchen. The timer can be useful to remind you when food needs to be turned, checked or taken off the grill.

■ A **meat thermometer** is a great aid as it helps you to achieve a perfectly cooked roast every time. The thermometer indicates the internal temperature of the meat being cooked. It should be inserted into the centre of the thickest part of the meat when you think the meat is cooked. Wait a few minutes and you can check the thermometer against the temperature on the cooking charts (see charts for poultry on pages 66-7 and meat on pages 88-9). Do not leave the thermometer in the meat during cooking.

■ A **foil drip pan** or metal dish lined with foil will keep the base of the barbecue clean by catching any fats, juices and bastes which fall from the food during cooking. When selecting a drip pan, it is important that it is large enough to catch all of the drippings from the food above.

■ **Skewers** are an excellent way of cooking meats or fish with vegetables and other flavourings such as bay leaves or chillies, all at the same time. They make life simple for the cook because kebabs can be prepared in advance and exact portions per person can be divided onto the skewers. It's also quicker and easier to rotate a few kebabs than spend time turning over individual meats or fish and a variety of vegetables. The choice of foods that can be skewered and cooked together are almost endless. Skewers come in various lengths and are made from different materials. Metal skewers are the most common and are good conductors of heat, helping the food cook in the centre. They are also reusable. Double prong skewers prevent food from turning on the skewer. Disposable wooden or bamboo skewers are also good but they must be soaked in cold water for at least 30 minutes before you use them.

Left: **A long handled brush is vital for cleaning the cooking grate each time you use your grill.**

Right: **Long handled equipment not only makes the job safer but also quicker and more efficient.**

marinades

Marinades enhance and can even improve the flavour of meats, fish or vegetables. Cheaper cuts of meat benefit greatly from a brief soaking in olive oil and a mixture of your favourite herbs or spices. In addition, marinades have an acidic ingredient such as lemon juice or vinegar, which helps tenderise the meat. Most marinades use an oil base which helps keep the meat or fish moist during cooking. To avoid flare-ups, brush off any excess before placing the food on the grill.

Where possible marinate food in a cool area and not the refrigerator as this tends to dull the flavour. If the food requires marinating for over 2 hours, or more, it's best to keep it chilled; just remember to bring it back to room temperature before cooking. Keep meat or fish covered during marinating and turn the pieces halfway through, to ensure the food has been covered equally all over. Do not use leftover marinade on the finished dish, as it has been in contact with the raw meat.

As a general guide cuts of meat and chicken will need about an hour while fish should flavour in about 30 minutes. Slashes or cuts applied to the meat or fish will help the flavours to penetrate and speed up the process.

Opposite top: **Classic Chinese marinade.**

Opposite centre: **Spiced ginger & yoghurt marinade.**

Opposite bottom: **Lemon, garlic & oregano marinade.**

The following recipes are for about 900 g/2 lb of meat or fish.

Fresh rosemary & garlic marinade

Use for lamb, beef, pork, veal, chicken, or turkey

150ml/¼ pint olive oil
2 tablespoons white wine vinegar
3 garlic cloves, roughly chopped
2 long stems fresh rosemary, sprigs removed and bruised
½ teaspoon roughly crushed peppercorns

Put all the ingredients into a bowl and mix together very well. Arrange the meat or chicken in a single layer in a shallow dish and pour over the marinade. Cover and marinate for 1 hour.

Lemon, garlic & oregano marinade

Use for lamb, pork, veal, chicken, turkey, or fish

150ml/¼ pint olive oil
1 lemon, juice and pared rind
1 large garlic clove, thinly sliced
2 tablespoons roughly torn fresh oregano
Salt and freshly ground black pepper

Mix all the ingredients well in a bowl. Arrange the raw food in a shallow dish and pour over the marinade. Cover and marinate meat or poultry for 1 hour, fish for 30 minutes.

Spiced ginger & yoghurt marinade

Use for lamb, chicken, duck, turkey, or fish

225g/8oz natural yoghurt
2 garlic cloves crushed
2.5cm/1inch piece of fresh ginger, grated
½ lemon, juice only
1 teaspoon ground cumin
1 teaspoon ground coriander
½ teaspoon crushed cardamom
½ teaspoon cayenne pepper
½ teaspoon salt
3 tablespoons roughly torn fresh mint

Pour the yoghurt into a bowl. Add all the other ingredients and stir together well. Arrange the meat, chicken or fish in a shallow dish and pour over the marinade. Cover and marinate meat or chicken for 1 hour, fish for 30 minutes, turning once.

Classic Chinese marinade

Use for beef, pork, chicken, duck, or fish

2 tablespoons rice wine vinegar
4 tablespoons soy sauce
1 tablespoon sesame oil
2 tablespoons liquid honey
2.5cm/1 inch piece fresh root ginger, grated
2 garlic cloves, roughly chopped
1 teaspoon five spice powder

Whisk the ingredients together in a bowl. Arrange the raw food in a single layer in a shallow dish and pour over the marinade. Cover and marinate meat or poultry for 1 hour, fish for 30 minutes.

Dill, horseradish & black peppercorn marinade

Use for beef or fish

6 tablespoons olive oil
6 tablespoons white wine vinegar
½ lemon, juice only
3 tablespoons chopped fresh dill
½ tablespoon fresh horseradish, grated
8 black peppercorns
¼ teaspoon salt

Put all the ingredients into a bowl and mix well. Arrange the beef or fish in a single layer in a shallow dish and pour over the marinade. Cover and marinate beef for 1 hour, fish for 30 minutes.

Dijon white wine marinade

Use for lamb, pork, beef, veal, chicken, turkey, or fish

2 tablespoons Dijon mustard
4 tablespoons white wine vinegar
4 tablespoons olive oil
1 shallot, finely chopped
1 garlic clove, finely chopped
Salt and freshly ground black pepper

Put all the ingredients into a bowl and mix together well. Arrange the meat, chicken or fish in a single layer in a shallow dish and pour over the marinade. Cover and marinate meat or chicken for 1 hour, fish for 30 minutes.

herb & spice rubs

Think of a 'rub' as a drier version of a marinade. While most marinades are oil based and work by seeping the flavour into the meat or fish, the spice or herb rub is, as the name implies, literally rubbed into the food before it's cooked. A splash of oil can also be added to herb and spice rubs to make them more paste like if you prefer. If you wish make shallow cuts in the food before applying the rub. Cover the meat or fish with the rub and leave to soak up the flavours for about an hour before cooking to give the best flavour results. If you are short on time herb and spice rubs have the advantage of being quicker than traditional marinades as the food absorbs the flavours more instantly and can be cooked straight away with good flavour results.

As most spice rubs are made with dry ingredients and are quick to put together, there is little point in making them in advance, but any left over will keep for several weeks stored in a sealed jar in a cool dry cupboard. The great joy in making spice and herb rubs is the endless combinations you can create. The following recipes will give you a good guideline as to the general quantities you will require, but after that, the larder or garden is your limit.

The following recipes yield enough rub mixture for about 900 g/2 lb of meat, poultry or fish.

Sweet & spicy barbecue rub

Use for lamb, pork, beef, veal, chicken, or turkey

2 teaspoons chilli powder
2 teaspoons paprika
3 teaspoons soft brown sugar
1 teaspoon ground cumin
1 teaspoon cayenne pepper
1 teaspoon mustard powder
2 teaspoons freshly ground black pepper
1 teaspoon garlic salt

Put all the ingredients into a bowl and mix together very well.

Cajun spice rub

Use for all meats, chicken, turkey or fish

2 teaspoons hot paprika
1 teaspoon dried thyme
1 teaspoon dried oregano
1 teaspoon black peppercorns
1 teaspoon white peppercorns
1 teaspoon onion powder
1 teaspoon garlic powder
1 teaspoon salt
1 teaspoon cumin seeds

Put all the ingredients into a mortar and pestle and grind to a fine powder.

Opposite top: **Lemon herb rub.**

Opposite centre: **Texas dry rub.**

Opposite bottom: **Moroccan spice rub.**

Lemon herb rub

Use for pork, chicken, turkey, or fish

4 large garlic cloves, crushed
1 lemon, grated rind only
2 teaspoons dried rosemary, chopped
1 teaspoon dried basil leaves, chopped
½ teaspoon salt
½ teaspoon dried thyme leaves, chopped
½ teaspoon freshly ground black pepper

Put all the ingredients into a bowl and mix well.

Texas dry rub

Use for lamb, pork, veal, chicken or turkey

1 garlic clove, crushed
1 teaspoon mustard seeds, crushed
1 tablespoon salt
1 teaspoon chilli powder
1 teaspoon cayenne pepper
1 teaspoon paprika
½ teaspoon ground coriander
½ teaspoon ground cumin

Put the garlic and mustard seeds into a mortar and pestle and grind to a paste. Add the remaining ingredients to the bowl and mix together well to form a dry rub.

Moroccan spice rub

Use for lamb, chicken, duck, turkey, or fish

1 teaspoon ground cumin
1 lemon, finely grated rind only
½ teaspoon saffron powder
1 teaspoon hot chilli powder
½ teaspoon ground coriander
2 tablespoons fresh coriander, finely chopped
1 garlic clove, finely chopped
¼ teaspoon sea salt
½ teaspoon freshly ground black pepper

Put all the ingredients into a mortar and pestle and rub or mix together thoroughly into a paste.

flavoured butters

Flavoured butters make brilliant instant 'sauces' for grilled meats, chicken or fish. A simple barbecued steak, chicken or fish fillet from the grill turns into a flavourful meal with the addition of your favourite butter. You can prepare them in advance and there are many flavours you can create by simply stirring together your choice of herbs, spices or flavourings into softened butter. Spoon the butter onto a large sheet of greaseproof paper, rolling up the butter inside the paper into a log shape, and secure the ends like a Christmas cracker. Chill in the fridge to firm up. To serve simply cut the log into thick slices and put a slice on the hot meat or fish as soon as it comes off the grill. Flavoured butters can be frozen to keep longer.

Coriander & orange butter

Use for beef, pork and fish

225g/8oz butter, softened
1 orange, grated rind only
2 tablespoons chopped fresh coriander

Beat all the ingredients together, roll up and chill until firm.

Provençal herb butter

Use for chicken, pork, lamb, fish and shellfish

1 teaspoon fresh thyme, chopped
1 teaspoon fresh marjoram, chopped
1 teaspoon fresh basil, chopped
1 teaspoon fresh oregano, chopped
225g/8oz butter, softened

Beat the fresh herbs into the butter, roll up and chill until firm.

Lemon & fennel butter

Use for chicken, pork, fish and shellfish

1 teaspoon fennel seeds
225g/8oz butter, softened
1 lemon, grated rind only
1 tablespoon chopped fresh fennel

Dry fry the fennel seeds in a small frying pan for 1 minute until they smell aromatic. Put into a mortar and pestle and roughly grind. Stir into the softened butter with the lemon rind and fresh fennel, roll up and chill until firm.

Three pepper butter

Use for beef, pork and fish

225g/8oz butter, softened
1 teaspoon pink peppercorns in brine, drained
1 teaspoon green peppercorns in brine, drained
1 teaspoon freshly ground black peppercorns

Beat all the ingredients together, roll up and chill until firm.

Roasted chilli butter

Use for beef, pork, vegetables and fish

5 large red chillies
1 tablespoon olive oil
2 tablespoons chopped fresh parsley
225g/8oz butter, softened

Put the chillies into a small roasting tray and brush with the oil. Roast in the oven at 230°C/450°F/Gas 8 for 10–15 minutes. Cool and scrape out the seeds then roughly chop the chillies. Beat into the butter with the parsley, roll up and chill until firm.

Right: **Roasted chilli butter.**

Whatever combination of ingredients you are using, make sure you beat them well into the butter before rolling and shaping.

appetizers

Food has always drawn people together. Give a dinner party and everyone will eventually end up in the kitchen, and barbecuing outside is no exception. As soon as the barbecue is lit people gather around it in anticipation; why not give them a little taste of things to come? People often push aside the notion of making appetizers or starters, believing that barbecuing one course is quite enough of a feat with an audience at hand. But with a little forethought and preparation you can pass around a platter of delicious hot appetizers that are irresistible, simple to cook and take no time at all to prepare. Tempt them with tiger prawns with hot sweet sauce, or whet their appetites with ginger and lemon chicken wings.

Mixed Satays
with peanut sauce

Gas	Direct/High heat	☀ ☀
Charcoal	Direct	
Prep time	40 minutes + 1 hour marinating	
Grilling time	6–8 minutes	Serves 4

1 tablespoon olive oil

1 small onion, chopped

2 red chillies, deseeded and chopped

3 tablespoons light soy sauce

1 tablespoon muscovado or brown sugar

1 lime, juice only

1 teaspoon curry paste

150g/5oz boneless skinless chicken breast

150g/5oz sirloin steak

150g/5oz pork tenderloin

Peanut sauce

1 tablespoon vegetable or peanut oil

1 garlic clove, finely crushed

1 teaspoon finely chopped lemon grass

5 tablespoons crunchy peanut butter

150ml/¼ pint coconut milk

1 lime, juice only

1 teaspoon muscovado or brown sugar

1 teaspoon chilli powder

Oil, for brushing

1 Soak 12 bamboo skewers in cold water for 30 minutes. Heat the olive oil in a small frying pan and cook the onion and chilli for 3–4 minutes until softened. Remove from the heat and add the soy sauce, sugar, lime juice and curry paste. Put aside to cool.

2 Cut the chicken, sirloin steak and pork tenderloin each into 4 strips. Put into a non-metallic bowl and pour over the marinade. Toss well and marinate, covered, for 1 hour at room temperature.

3 To make the **peanut sauce**, heat the oil in a saucepan and cook the garlic and lemon grass for 2 minutes until softened. Add the peanut butter, coconut milk, lime juice, chilli powder and sugar; simmer gently for 2–3 minutes until thickened. Keep warm.

4 Remove the strips of chicken and meat from the marinade and thread onto the skewers. Discard marinade. Brush the meat with a little oil. Barbecue over Direct High heat for 6–8 minutes on both sides, turning once. Serve with the warm peanut sauce.

The acidity of the lime juice in the marinade will act as a natural tenderiser for the meat and chicken.

The delicate flavour of the lemon grass in the peanut sauce helps to lighten the richness of the peanuts.

Garlic Prawns
wrapped in prosciutto

Gas	Direct/Medium heat	☀
Charcoal	Direct	
Prep time	15 minutes	
Grilling time	6 minutes	Serves 12

24 large prawns, peeled and deveined
2 garlic cloves, finely chopped
1 tablespoon chopped fresh dill or ½ teaspoon dried dill
1 tablespoon chopped fresh tarragon
  or ½ teaspoon dried tarragon
12 slices prosciutto
1 tablespoon olive oil
Salt and freshly ground black pepper

1 If using bamboo skewers soak in cold water for at least 30 minutes. Wash and dry the prawns. Put into a bowl with the garlic, dill, tarragon, salt, pepper and olive oil. (As prosciutto can be quite salty, season lightly). Toss well to coat. Cut prosciutto slices in half lengthwise. Wrap each prawn in a half-slice of prosciutto.

2 Thread the prawns onto skewers, leaving a little space between each. Barbecue over Direct Medium heat for 5–6 minutes, turning once halfway through grilling time, until the prawns are pink and firm. Serve hot from the grill.

Tiger Prawns
with hot sweet sauce

Gas	Direct/Medium heat	☀ ☀
Charcoal	Direct	
Prep time	25 minutes + 25 mins marinating	
Grilling time	2–3 minutes	Serves 4

16 tiger prawns, peeled and deveined
1 garlic clove, finely chopped
2 tablespoons olive oil
Salt and freshly ground black pepper

Hot sweet sauce
1 garlic clove, crushed
2 tablespoons light soy sauce
3 tablespoons liquid honey
1 lime, grated rind and juice
2 tablespoons fresh coriander, roughly chopped
1 teaspoon chilli flakes

1 Cut 8 bamboo skewers to 10cm/4 inches in length. Soak in cold water for at least 30 minutes. Rinse prawns and pat dry on kitchen paper. Put into a bowl with the chopped garlic and olive oil. Season well and toss. Cover and leave to marinate for 15 minutes.

2 To make the **hot sweet sauce**, put the crushed garlic, soy sauce, honey, grated rind of the whole lime and the juice of half the lime, coriander and chilli flakes in a bowl. Whisk together until the honey has dissolved into the other ingredients. Put into a small dish for dipping.

3 Thread two prawns onto each skewer. Barbecue over Direct Medium heat for 2–3 minutes, turning once halfway through grilling time, until pink and tender. Serve warm with the sauce.

Tiger prawns
See picture at bottom right
on page 30

Chicken Wings
with ginger & lemon

Gas	Indirect/Medium heat	✹ ✹
Charcoal	Indirect	
Prep time	20 minutes	
Grilling time	30 minutes	Serves 6

1 piece of stem ginger preserved in sugar syrup
5 tablespoons liquid honey
2 tablespoons dry sherry
1 lemon, grated rind and juice
Salt and freshly ground black pepper
12 large chicken wings, tips removed
Oil, for brushing

1 Cut the piece of ginger into fine strips and put into a small bowl. Add 1 tablespoon of the syrup taken from the jar.

2 Add the honey, sherry, lemon rind and juice and mix until all the ingredients are well blended. Put into a small saucepan and bring to the boil and cook for 3–4 minutes until reduced by half. Leave aside to cool.

3 Thread the chicken wings onto parallel pairs of metal skewers like the rungs of a ladder, or use double prong skewers (this makes them easier to turn during cooking).

4 Brush the wings on all sides with a little oil. Place in the middle of the cooking grate and barbecue over Indirect Medium heat for 20 minutes turning once. Brush with the ginger and lemon sauce and barbecue for another 10 minutes, turning once and brushing the other side with the sauce. Serve warm.

Bruschetta
with tomatoes & anchovies

Gas	Direct/Medium heat	✹
Charcoal	Direct	
Prep time	15 minutes	
Grilling time	5–6 minutes	Serves 6

6 small plum tomatoes
2 tablespoons olive oil
6 x 1 inch thick slices of baguette
1 large garlic clove
2 tablespoons tapenade or black olive paste
6 large basil leaves
12 fresh or canned anchovy fillets
Freshly ground black pepper
Olive oil, for drizzling

1 Cut the plum tomatoes in quarters and brush with a little oil. Barbecue over Direct Medium heat for 5–6 minutes, cut side up, until skin is slightly charred. Remove and put aside. Barbecue the bread slices over Direct Medium heat for 2–3 minutes, turning once until just toasted, and remove from the grill.

2 Immediately rub each toast slice with the garlic clove. Divide the tapenade between the bruschettas and top each with 2 tomato halves, a basil leaf and 2 anchovy fillets. Season with a little freshly ground black pepper. Drizzle with a little extra olive oil.

Bruschetta
See picture at top right on page 30

Aubergine Rolls
with goat's cheese and raita

Gas	Direct/Medium heat	☀ ☀
Charcoal	Direct	
Prep time	20 minutes	
Grilling time	4 minutes	Serves 8

2 aubergines
4 tablespoons olive oil, for brushing
175g/6oz goat's cheese
3 tablespoons fresh sage, chopped

Raita
11oz/300g natural yoghurt
2 garlic cloves, crushed
4 tablespoons fresh mint, chopped

1 Soak 16 cocktail sticks in cold water for 30 minutes. Using a sharp knife top and tail the aubergines and cut each lengthways into eight slices. Brush each slice with oil on both sides. Season well. Barbecue over Direct Medium heat for 6 minutes, turning once, until tender. Put aside to cool.

2 Meanwhile, to make the **raita**, put the yoghurt into a bowl and stir in the garlic and mint. Season well and chill until required. The raita can also be prepared in advance and kept chilled.

3 Cut the goat's cheese into 16 pieces. Lay a piece of goat's cheese on top of a slice of aubergine and scatter with a little chopped sage. Roll up and secure with a cocktail stick.

4 Barbecue the aubergine rolls over Indirect Low heat for 4 minutes, turning once.

5 Serve the warm aubergine rolls with the bowl of raita for dipping.

Grilled Oysters
in buttery barbecue sauce

Gas	Direct/High heat	☀
Charcoal	Direct	
Prep time	10 minutes	
Grilling time	5 minutes	Serves 3

12 fresh oysters

Barbecue sauce
1 tablespoon unsalted butter
1 teaspoon minced garlic
2 tablespoons freshly squeezed lemon juice
2 tablespoons mild chilli sauce

1 To make the barbecue sauce, sauté the butter and garlic in a saucepan over medium heat, stirring occasionally until the garlic aroma is apparent and the butter begins to brown, about 2 to 3 minutes. Remove the garlic butter from the heat and add the lemon juice and chilli sauce. Mix until well blended.

2 To open the oysters: grip each oyster flat side up in a folded kitchen towel. Find a small opening between the shells near the hinge and prise open with an oyster knife. Try to keep the juices in the shell. Loosen the oyster from the shell by running the oyster knife carefully underneath the body. Discard the top, flatter shell, keeping the oyster in the bottom, deeper shell.

3 Spoon ½ teaspoon of barbecue sauce over each oyster. Barbecue the oysters over Direct High heat, until the sauce boils inside the shell, after 2 to 3 minutes, then barbecue oysters for 1 to 2 minutes more. Serve warm.

Above Left: **Aubergine rolls.**

Above Right: **Grilled oysters.**

Grip the oyster knife carefully as
the shell may slip when you prise
open the oyster shell.

Minted Courgettes
with hummus

Gas	Direct/Medium heat	✳ ✳
Charcoal	Direct	
Prep time	30 minutes	
Grilling time	8 minutes	Serves 8–10

Hummus

225g/8oz can chickpeas
2 garlic cloves, roughly chopped
45ml/3 tablespoons lemon juice
60ml/4 tablespoons tahini paste
75ml/5 tablespoons olive oil
1 teaspoon ground cumin
Salt and freshly ground black pepper

Minted courgettes

1 tablespoon fresh mint, chopped
675g/1½lb medium-sized courgettes, trimmed
Oil, for brushing
10 black olives, quartered
Cayenne pepper

1 To make the **hummus**, drain and rinse the chickpeas and reserve the liquid from the can. Put into a food processor and blend to a smooth purée adding 1–2 tablespoons of the reserved liquid from the can.

2 Add the garlic, lemon juice and tahini paste, and process again until smooth. Still using the blender, gradually pour in 45ml/3 tablespoons olive oil. Add the cumin, season well and blend briefly. Chill until required. In a large bowl, mix the remaining olive oil with the chopped mint and leave aside.

3 To make the **minted courgettes**, cut the courgettes in half lengthways and brush with oil. Barbecue over Direct Medium heat for 8 minutes until tender, turning once . Remove from the heat and cut each courgette half into three pieces. Put into the bowl with the oil and mint and toss well. Season and leave to cool.

4 Top each piece of courgette with a spoonful of hummus. Garnish with black olives and a sprinkling of cayenne pepper. Arrange on a platter and serve cold.

When you turn the courgettes after about 3 to 4 minutes, the cut side should have distinct grill marks which give a delicious flavour.

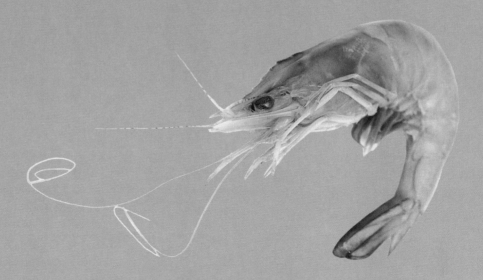

fish & shellfish

Nothing captures the true spirit of outdoor cooking as much as an open fire with the sizzling aroma of fresh fish or shellfish. Some outdoor cooks see fish as difficult and time consuming when in fact quite the opposite is true.

Small whole fish and shellfish are nature's real gift to the barbecue, and there's little to be done in preparation before the effortless task of grilling them.

Take a flavour journey of the world and sample classics such as Japanese fish steaks – teriyaki style, Scandinavian mackerel with a tangy dill, caper and tomato dressing, and an Australian signature dish of prawn and scallop skewers.

perfect fish

When choosing fish for the barbecue it is important to remember to select fish suitable for grilling and to choose the freshest fish available. Have a couple of options in mind for grilling – it makes good sense to buy the freshest catch of the day even if it is not your first choice. Fresh fish is easy to recognise. It should have a wonderful aroma of the sea and not a strong 'fishy' smell, and the eyes should be bright and clear. Lift up the gill cover and check the gills, which should be bright pink (not dull or red). Finally, the scales should be shiny and tight around the fish. Fishmongers with a high turnover are the best place to buy fish because you can choose the fish whole and check for these qualities, then you can ask them to gut and fillet the fish. Remember if you are grilling fish whole it will need to be gutted and the scales and fins removed. (Whether to grill with the head on or off is up to you.)

Flavouring fish

Whether you are cooking fish whole or in fillets, flavours can be incorporated in a variety of ways. For whole fish it is best to apply three or four deep slashes to both sides of the fish before marinating, or simply stuffing with lemon, lime or herbs. Flavoured butters can also be stuffed into the slashes but you will need to wrap and seal the fish in foil for grilling in order to keep in the melting butter. Fillets are best marinated or brushed with a sauce or glaze a few minutes before the end of the grilling time.

Good flavours with fish and shellfish

Tarragon ■ dill ■ fennel ■ oregano ■ basil ■ coriander ■ mint ■ chilli ■ ginger ■ coconut ■ capers ■ soy sauce ■ sesame oil ■ mustard ■ lemon ■ lime ■ mushroom ■ spring onion ■ white wine.

Grilling fish

■ **Whole fish** can be grilled directly on the cooking grate but to prevent the skin sticking it must be well oiled. You may even prefer to lay the fish on a piece of heavy-duty foil on the grate. To cook whole fish with other flavours, wrap in foil and seal well around the edges to keep in the juices.

■ **Firm fish fillets and fish steaks** can be grilled directly on a well-oiled cooking grate. Delicate fish fillets that flake easily should be placed on a piece of heavy-duty foil with the edges crimped to form shallow sides to keep in juices. You can add a little fish stock or wine to help keep the fish moist.

■ **To check fish is cooked through to the centre,** insert the tip of a knife into the thickest part of the fish then remove and carefully check if the tip is hot, or pull the flesh apart slightly which will give easily if the flesh is cooked through.

Most cuts of fresh fish are a great vehicle for other flavours, such as these salmon steaks, marinated with the Thai flavours of chilli, lemon grass, garlic and lime juice (see recipe page 50).

Fish and shellfish kebabs

Considering the wonderful array of fish there are few which are suitable for kebabs because most fish flakes easily when it's grilled and is liable to fall of the skewer. However, denser fish that work well are monkfish, tuna, halibut and turbot. Most shellfish, which have a dense texture, are good in kebabs, and appropriate ones include tiger prawns, langoustine and shelled scallops.

Safety points

- Fish and shellfish should always have a pleasant smell of the sea and not a strong fishy smell.

- Keep all fresh fish well refrigerated. It's best to grill fish on the day of purchase.

- Wash fish well before preparing and grilling.

- When preparing mussels, clams and scallops ensure they are all tightly closed. Any that are open should be tapped sharply with the back of a knife and, if they do not close, should be discarded immediately. Similarly, discard any that have not opened after cooking.

- Thoroughly wash your hands, utensils, chopping boards and work surfaces after preparing raw fish and shellfish. Raw fish is not necessarily unsafe but it can contaminate the flavours of other foods easily.

What could be more apt or easier than fish steaks grilled at the beach ?

perfect shellfish

Grilling shellfish

■ **Prawns** can be cooked with or without their tail shells, but either way you will need to devein them first. Unless the recipe calls for whole prawns, pull off the heads and discard. If leaving the tail shell on, run a sharp knife down the back of the shell, cutting through the shell and about 5mm/¼ inch into the flesh. Use a cocktail stick to pick out the black line running along the back and discard. If grilling the prawns unshelled, simple pull off the shell first before deveining in the same way. Shelled prawns are best skewered first for easy turning.

■ **Lobsters** should be cut in half lengthways using a large chopping knife. Remove and discard the large dark vein running down the length of the tail. Crack the claws with the back of a large knife. Barbecue over Direct Medium heat, flesh side down, for 30 seconds to 1 minute to seal in juices. Turn over and grill for a further 8–10 minutes until flesh is firm and shells are bright red. Serve with lemon wedges and slices of flavoured butter.

■ **Mussels and Clams** can be wrapped in 450g/1lb portions in large sheets of heavy-duty foil with butter, wine and herbs and barbecued over Indirect Medium heat until they open. Discard any shellfish which remain closed.

■ **Scallops** should be opened by inserting the blade of a sharp knife between the shells and severing the muscle. Discard one half of the shell. Clean and remove the greyish outer frill, leaving just the coral and scallop in the remaining half of the shell. These can be placed directly on the cooking grate over Direct Medium heat and grilled for 6–8 minutes until tender. Alternatively, you can remove the scallop and coral completely from the shell, skewer and grill directly on the oiled cooking grate.

■ **Oysters** can be prepared and grilled in one half of their shells in the same way as scallops, but they only need about 1–2 minutes grilling time after their juices have come to the boil. Razor clams can also be grilled in this way. (See page 36 for instructions on how to prepare oysters for grilling.)

■ **Squid** are not technically shellfish but are often grouped in this category. The cleaned flesh should be lightly scored with a knife and threaded onto a skewer to prevent it curling up when grilling. Barbecue over Direct High heat for 2–3 minutes until just tender.

cook's guide to fish & shellfish

Fish for the barbecue falls into three categories: fish fillets, whole fish and shellfish. Generally fish fillets, small cuts (kebabs) and shellfish should be barbecued over Direct heat and large whole fish over Indirect heat for the times indicated. Use heavy-duty tin foil under any fish that is quite flaky when cooked, or whole fillets of fish, such as a side of salmon. Place the fish on the foil and bring it around the sides of the fish like a shallow tray. Fish barbecued in this way should not be turned during cooking.

Most fish can be cooked on the barbecue but, for a true barbecue flavour and appearance, some varieties will work better than others. Fish such as cod and haddock are impossible to turn and should be supported by heavy-duty tin foil because they flake and fall apart easily. While they can be cooked in this fashion some of the charred flavour and the blackened grill marks traditionally associated with barbecuing or grilling are sacrificed.

Remember that, unless it's a very firm fleshed fish like monkfish or tuna, it can break up unless it's supported by it's own skin and bones. Hence a lot of fish is cooked whole, but even some of these need to be treated with care or they can stick and break on the cooking grate. Always oil the cooking grate and the fish well before grilling. A general rule for grilling fish is 4–5 minutes for ½ inch thickness and 8–10 minutes for 1 inch thickness.

Right: Making a shallow tray with heavy duty foil is ideal for whole sides of large fish such as salmon. It enables you to remove the barbecued fish from the grill without risk of it flaking and breaking up.

Good fish fillets for grilling
Salmon ■ sea bass ■ monkfish (best cut into chunks and skewered) ■ halibut ■ turbot.

Good fish steaks for grilling
Salmon ■ tuna ■ swordfish.

Good whole fish for grilling
Mackerel ■ red and grey mullet ■ bream ■ sea bass ■ trout (fresh water and sea) ■ dover sole ■ sardines ■ herring.

Shellfish
Lobster ■ crab ■ tiger prawns ■ langoustine ■ scallops ■ mussels ■ clams ■ squid.

Fish & Shellfish

To check when a fillet is perfectly cooked (usually at the point when the centre is just changing from translucent to opaque) cut it open to see. With experience you will know whether it is done just by touch, generally the flesh will be firm and will just give slightly when ready. Shellfish only take a few minutes on the grill; wherever possible, grill them with the shells on to retain their juices.

Type of fish or shellfish to be grilled	Weight	Cooking time
Fish fillets	1cm/½inch thick	3–5 minutes
	2cm/¾ inch thick	5–10 minutes
Fish steaks	2.5cm/1 inch thick	10–12 minutes
Fish kebabs	2.5cm/1 inch thick	8–10 minutes
Whole fish and fillets	2.5cm/1 inch thick	8–10 minutes
	4cm/1½ inch thick	10–15 minutes
	5–6cm/2–2½ inch thick/1lb	15–20 minutes
	7.5cm/3 inch thick/1–2lb	20–30 minutes
	or 2–4lb	30–45 minutes
Crab	approx. 1.2kg/2½lb	10–12 minutes
Whole Lobster	approx. 900g/2lb	18–20 minutes
Lobster tails	225–275 g/8–10oz	8–12 minutes
Prawns (Tiger/Langoustine) with shells	medium size	4–5 minutes
	large size	5–6 minutes
	extra large size	6–8 minutes
Prawns (Tiger/Langoustine) without shells take about 1–2 minutes less than the above timings		
Scallops, without shells	2.5–5cm/1–2 inches diameter	4–6 minutes
Clams	medium size	5–8 minutes
Oysters	small size	3–6 minutes
Mussels	medium size	4–5 minutes

Thai Salmon
with Pad Thai noodles

Gas	Direct/Medium heat	
Charcoal	Direct	✳ ✳ ✳
Prep time	25 minutes + 30 mins marinating	
Grilling time	6–8 minutes	Serves 4

4 salmon fillets or salmon steaks, about 225g/8oz each
  in weight
1 garlic clove, crushed
1 lemon grass stem, chopped
2 red chillies, deseeded and sliced
1 lime, juice only
2 tablespoons Thai fish sauce
4 tablespoons sunflower oil

Pad Thai noodles
225g/8oz sen lek Thai noodles (flat flour noodles)
2 tablespoons peanut oil
2 tablespoons sunflower oil
1 garlic clove, chopped
1 shallot, chopped
1 red chilli, deseeded and finely shredded
2 tablespoons Thai fish sauce
1 lime, juice only
1 teaspoon brown sugar
Small bunch spring onions, finely shredded
50g/2oz roasted peanuts, roughly chopped
50g/2oz bean sprouts
2 tablespoons chopped fresh coriander

1 Put the salmon into a large shallow dish in a single layer. In a small bowl mix the crushed garlic, lemon grass, sliced chillies, lime juice, Thai fish sauce and sunflower oil. Pour over the salmon and leave to marinate, covered, in a cool place for 30 minutes.

2 Meanwhile, to make the **Pad Thai noodles**, cook the noodles in boiling salted water according to the packet instructions until tender. Drain and refresh under cold running water. Drain again. Heat the peanut and sunflower oils in a wok, add the chopped garlic and shallot and fry for 1–2 minutes until just golden. Add the chilli, fish sauce, lime juice and sugar, cooking for 30 seconds, and remove from heat. Toss with the noodles, half the spring onions, bean sprouts and peanuts. Put aside.

Have all the ingredients ready to toss with the noodles at the last minute, to keep the flavours and textures as crisp as possible.

3 Scrape excess marinade off the salmon steaks and barbecue them over Direct Medium heat for 6–8 minutes, turning once halfway through grilling time.

4 Sprinkle the coriander and the remaining spring onions over the Pad Thai noodles. Serve with the hot salmon steaks.

Cook's note

If lemon grass is unavailable use the pared rind of a lemon in the marinade – this will give a similar flavour. For a simpler variation of this recipe, replace the Pad Thai noodles with plain rice.

Whole Fish
cooked with Charmoula butter

Gas	Direct/Medium heat	✳ ✳ ✳
Charcoal	Direct	
Prep time	30 minutes	
Grilling time	15 minutes	Serves 4

Charmoula butter

175g/6oz butter, softened
2 tablespoons chopped fresh coriander
3 garlic cloves, finely chopped
1½ teaspoons ground cumin
1½ teaspoons paprika
½ red chilli, deseeded and chopped
½ teaspoon saffron strands
1 lemon, grated rind
Salt and freshly ground black pepper

4 whole fish, weighing about 450g/1lb each
4 spring onions, sliced
Lemon wedges, to serve

1 Make the **charmoula butter** by putting the softened butter into a large bowl with the coriander, garlic, cumin, paprika, chilli, saffron, grated rind of the lemon and seasoning. Beat with a wooden spoon until well combined.

2 Wash the fish under cold running water and scrape off the scales from head to tail using a blunt knife. Cut off the fins. Using a sharp knife make three or four deep cuts in the flesh on each side of the fish.

3 Lay each fish in the centre of a large square of tin foil. Spread the charmoula butter over each fish making sure some of the butter goes into the cuts (you only need to spread the butter on one side of the fish).

4 Cut the grated lemon into eight neat wedges and arrange two on top of each fish. Scatter each fish with the sliced spring onions and wrap in the foil, sealing well.

5 Put the four parcels on the cooking grate and barbecue over Direct Medium heat for 12–15 minutes, until tender. Divide the parcels between plates with extra lemon wedges and let each person open their own parcel so they can appreciate the wonderful aroma.

Aussie Prawn
& scallop skewers

Gas	Indirect/Medium heat	✳ ✳
Charcoal	Indirect	
Prep time	5 minutes	
Grilling time	6–8 minutes	Serves 4

175g/6oz mango chutney
120ml/4fl oz orange juice
115g/4oz sweet and tangy barbecue sauce
8 baby onions or shallots
8 fresh pineapple chunks, about 2.5cm/1 inch
12 large raw prawns, peeled and deveined
12 large scallops
8 cherry tomatoes
Salt and pepper

1 Soak four bamboo skewers in cold water for 30 minutes. Put the mango chutney, orange juice and barbecue sauce into a food processor or blender and blend until smooth. Set aside.

2 Put the onions or shallots into a small saucepan and cover with water. Bring to the boil and simmer for 1 minute then drain and refresh immediately under cold running water. When cool enough to handle, peel and set aside.

3 Thread the pineapple, prawns, scallops, tomatoes and onion (or shallots) onto the skewers. Season and brush liberally with the reserved sauce. Barbecue over Indirect Medium heat for 6–8 minutes, or until the prawns and scallops are tender, turning once and brushing with sauce. Serve with remaining sauce for dipping.

Right: **Aussie prawn and scallop skewers.**

◀ ***Cook's note***

The Whole Fish recipe will work for most small whole fish weighing about 350g–450g/12oz–1lb. Try red snapper, sea bass, sea bream, talaipere, trout, sole or plaice but avoid oily fish such as mackerel or herring. Once the fish is gutted and thoroughly washed, scrape off the scales and cut off the fins to make eating the whole fish easier. Making deep cuts in the flesh will help the flavoured butter to penetrate.

Grilled Sardines
with chilli & lemon dressing

Gas	Direct/Medium heat	
Charcoal	Direct	
Prep time	20 minutes + marinating	☀
Grilling time	6–10 minutes	Serves 4

4 tablespoons olive oil

5 shallots thinly sliced

125ml/4fl oz white wine vinegar

4 garlic cloves, crushed

Large handful mint leaves, chopped

1 lemon, juice and zest

½ teaspoon chilli flakes

Salt and freshly ground black pepper

675g/1½lb fresh sardines, gutted

Oil, for brushing

1 Heat 1 tablespoon olive oil in a saucepan, add the shallots and cook for 3–4 minutes until softened. Add the vinegar and bring to the boil, then reduce the heat and simmer until reduced by half.

2 Add the remaining olive oil, garlic, mint, lemon zest and juice, chillies and seasoning and cook for a further 1 minute. Remove from heat and put aside.

3 Cut the tails and fins from the sardines (if you like) and wash well. Pat dry with kitchen paper. Brush the cooking grate with a little oil. Season the sardines and barbecue over Direct Medium heat for 4–10 minutes (see cook's note) turning once until tender. Arrange on a platter and pour over the cooled dressing.

Cook's note

Sardines can vary greatly in size, so cooking times will differ. If they are about 5–10cm/2–4 inches cook for 4–6 minutes turning once. For sardines up to 20cm/8 inches long, cook for about 6–10 minutes turning once.

Left: **Grilled sardines.**

Salt-crusted Prawns
with oregano dipping sauce

Gas	Direct/Medium heat	
Charcoal	Direct	
Prep time	25 minutes	☀
Grilling time	6–8 minutes	Serves 4

Oregano dipping sauce

120ml/4 fl oz extra virgin olive oil

1 lemon, juice only

50ml/2 fl oz boiling water

2 garlic cloves, crushed

1 teaspoon dried oregano

2 tablespoons chopped fresh parsley

Salt-crusted prawns

500g/1¼lb large whole raw prawns

3 tablespoons olive oil

65g/2½oz sea salt

1 For the **oregano dipping sauce**, whisk together the extra virgin olive oil, lemon juice and hot water. Stir in the garlic, oregano and parsley. Set aside for 20 minutes for the flavours to develop.

2 Meanwhile, prepare the **salt-crusted prawns**. Use a small knife to make a slit down the backs of the prawns and remove the vein, but do not remove the shells.

3 Put the prawns in a large bowl and toss with the olive oil to coat. Add the salt and mix well, ensuring that each prawn gets a good coating of salt. Thread 2 or 3 prawns at a time onto wooden skewers, to help turn them while they are grilling.

4 Barbecue the prawns over Direct Medium heat for 6–8 minutes, turning once, until tender. Serve warm with the oregano dipping sauce.

Salt-crusted prawns
See picture at bottom right on page 42 and on page 46

Salmon Fillets
with basil & mint crème

Gas	Direct/Medium heat	✳ ✳	
Charcoal	Direct		
Prep time	30 minutes		
Grilling time	8 minutes		Serves 4

25g/1oz fresh basil leaves

25g/1oz fresh mint leaves

200ml/7fl oz light olive oil

1 egg yolk

1 teaspoon Dijon mustard

Salt and freshly ground black pepper

1 lime, finely grated rind and juice

2 tablespoons crème fraiche

4 salmon fillets with skin on, about 225g/8oz each in weight

Oil, for brushing

1 Bring a pan of water to the boil and add the basil and mint leaves for 15 seconds. Remove the herbs and drain well; absorb excess water on kitchen paper. Put into a food processor with the olive oil and blend well. Leave aside for 15 minutes to infuse.

2 Put the egg yolk, mustard and plenty of seasoning into a bowl and whisk until smooth. Gradually blend in the basil and mint olive oil a trickle at a time until all the oil is added and the mixture is thick and smooth. Whisk in the lime juice and rind, stir in the crème fraiche, then chill.

3 Brush the salmon fillets with oil and barbecue skin side down over Direct Medium heat for 4 minutes. Brush with a little more oil, then turn over and cook for a further 4 minutes. Serve hot with the basil and mint crème.

Teriyaki Fish Steaks
with green & black rice

Gas	Direct/Medium heat	✳ ✳ ✳	
Charcoal	Direct		
Prep time	25 minutes + 30 mins marinating		
Grilling time	6 minutes		Serves 4

3 tablespoons sake (Japanese rice wine)

3 tablespoons dry sherry

3 tablespoons dark soy sauce

1½ tablespoon soft brown sugar

4 fish steaks, about 175–200g/6–7oz each in weight

Green & black rice

Salt

350g/12oz long-grain and wild rice

2.5cm/1 inch piece of fresh ginger

225g/8oz mange tout

Small bunch spring onions, cut into fine strips

1 Put the sake, sherry, soy sauce and brown sugar into a small saucepan and heat until the sugar dissolves, then bring to the boil and remove from the heat. Leave to cool.

2 Put the fish steaks into a shallow dish in a single layer and pour over the cold teriyaki sauce. Leave to marinate, covered, for 30 minutes in a cool place (not the fridge), turning once.

3 Meanwhile, to make the **green and black rice**, bring a large pan of salted water to the boil and add the piece of ginger and the long grain and wild rice. Cook according to packet instruction until just tender. Cut each mange tout lengthways into 3 or 4 strips and cook in boiling salted water for 2 minutes. Drain and refresh under cold running water. Drain the rice, remove the ginger and discard. Stir the mange tout and spring onions into the hot rice.

4 Remove the steaks from the marinade and barbecue over Direct Medium heat for 5–6 minutes, turning once and brushing a few times with the reserved teriyaki sauce. Serve with the hot green and black rice.

Cook's note

This recipe will adapt to suit any kind of firm fleshed fish that's suitable for cutting into steaks, such as tuna, swordfish, salmon, turbot or halibut. Monkfish is also wonderful when cooked teriyaki style but is best cut into bite size pieces first and skewered.

Above Left: **Salmon steaks.**

Above Right: **Teriyaki fish steaks.**

Right: **An infusion of basil and mint will complement the delicate flavour of the grilled salmon.**

Left: **The fish steaks will keep succulent if brushed with teriyaki sauce during grilling.**

Fish & Shellfish **57**

When slashing the mackerel to insert the sprigs of dill, be sure not to cut right through the fish, as it may disintegrate too easily during grilling.

Cook's note

The dill, caper and tomato dressing is based on a traditional Scandinavian recipe. The reaction of the tomato mixture with the oil and vinegar gives a pretty mottled effect to the dressing.

Grilled Mackerel
with tangy dill dressing

Gas	Direct/Medium heat	✻ ✻ ✻
Charcoal	Direct	
Prep time	40 minutes	
Grilling time	12 minutes	Serves 4

4 gutted mackerel
A small bunch fresh dill
Oil, for brushing

Dill dressing
1 lemon
2 tablespoons olive oil
1 small onion, chopped
1 garlic clove, crushed
200g/7oz can chopped tomatoes
1 teaspoon caster sugar
4 tablespoons red wine vinegar
120ml/4fl oz extra virgin olive oil
2 tablespoons fresh chives, chopped
2 tablespoons capers, drained
Salt and freshly ground black pepper

1 Wash the mackerel under cold running water and cut off the fins. Make three or four deep slashes through to the bone in each side of the mackerel. Stuff each slash with a small sprig of dill and leave aside. Chop remaining dill and reserve.

2 To make the **dill dressing**, heat the olive oil in a small saucepan and cook the onion and garlic for 2–3 minutes until softened. Add the chopped tomatoes and simmer for 10–15 minutes. Meanwhile in a small clean saucepan put 2 tablespoons vinegar and the sugar and boil rapidly until reduced to about 2 teaspoonfuls. Combine with the tomato mixture and stir in well.

3 Press the tomato mixture through a sieve and return to a clean saucepan and cook for 1–2 minutes until thickened. Leave the mixture to cool.

4 Put 2 tablespoons vinegar into a bowl with the olive oil, the chopped dill, chives, and seasoning and whisk well. Stir the tomato mixture and capers into the herb vinaigrette.

5 Brush the mackerel with a little oil. Barbecue over Direct Medium heat for 10–12 minutes until tender, turning once halfway through cooking time. Serve hot with the cool dressing.

Grilled Mussels
with Pernod & fennel butter

Gas	Indirect/Medium heat	❋ ❋
Charcoal	Indirect	
Prep time	20 minutes	
Grilling time	10–12 minutes	Serves 4

1.75g/4–4½lb mussels
175g /6oz butter, softened
2 tablespoons Pernod
1 tablespoons fresh fennel, chopped
1 tablespoons fresh chives, chopped
2 garlic cloves, crushed
Fennel sprigs to garnish

1 Wash and scrub the mussels under cold running water and remove the tough fibrous beard protruding from between the firmly closed shells. (Discard any shells that are open and refuse to shut when lightly tapped with a knife.) Leave aside.

2 Put the butter, Pernod, fennel, chives and garlic into a large bowl and beat well.

3 Take two large sheets of heavy duty tin foil and lay one on top of the other. Put a quarter of the mussels in the middle, dotting them with a quarter of the butter. Bring the sides of the foil up around the mussels to form a bowl shape, then bring the edges of the foil together and seal to form a loose parcel. Repeat with more foil and the remaining mussels and butter to make four parcels in all.

4 Place parcels on the cooking grate and barbecue over Indirect Medium heat for 10–12 minutes until all the mussels have opened. (Throw away any mussels that have not opened.) Serve garnished with a sprig of fennel.

Crab Fishcakes
with chilli dipping sauce

Gas	Direct/Medium heat	❋ ❋
Charcoal	Direct	
Prep time	30 minutes + 1 hour chilling	
Grilling time	7–8 minutes	Serves 6

175g/6oz firm white fish, such as cod, hake or haddock
250g/9oz fresh or canned white crab meat
125g/4oz can sweetcorn, drained
1 red chilli, deseeded and chopped
2 spring onions, finely chopped
2 tablespoons fresh coriander, chopped
1 tablespoons Thai fish sauce
1 egg, beaten
Salt and freshly ground black pepper
Oil, for brushing

Chilli dipping sauce
6 tablespoons rice wine vinegar
1 teaspoon caster sugar
1 birds eye chilli, sliced

1 Remove any skin and bones from the white fish. Cut the flesh into pieces and put into a food processor and blend for a few seconds until a paste is formed. Scrape out and put into a bowl. Stir in the crab meat.

2 Add to the sweetcorn, chilli, spring onion, coriander, fish sauce, egg and seasoning. Mix together very well until all the ingredients are well combined.

3 Divide the mixture into twelve parts and shape each into a round cake about 2cm/¾ inch thick. Put on a tray and chill for at least 1 hour to firm up.

4 Meanwhile, to make the **chilli dipping sauce**, mix the rice wine vinegar, caster sugar and chilli together. Put aside.

4 Brush the cakes with oil and barbecue over Direct Medium heat for 7–8 minutes turning once halfway through cooking time, until browned. Serve with chilli dipping sauce.

Right: **Crab fishcakes.**

poultry

A plump, juicy chicken, turkey or duck with seared crispy skin is the hero of the barbecue. These brilliant and versatile meats are suitable for a host of fascinating and diverse recipes – make it spicy with hot flavours from Mexico and India, or try the sweet and sour tastes of China and Thailand. And to enjoy ingredients closer to home, try soft-scented herbs or the sharp zing of lemon and lime.

Lock flavours in by stuffing red peppers beneath the skin of chicken legs before grilling, or marinate with aromatic spices. Learn how to prepare and cook a whole duck that grills to perfection with its own delicious fruit chutney hidden inside, or poussin glazed in apple jelly. In no time, you'll be tempted to roll out the barbecue at Easter or Christmas to cook a whole turkey flavoured with orange and thyme that's as succulent and moist as any that you've served from a conventional oven.

perfect poultry

When it comes to poultry, we are spoiled for choice. There are handy packed portions or whole oven ready birds ranging from corn-fed, free range or organic. Think about how you plan to prepare and cook your chicken before buying. If you intend to marinate with strong flavours or spices you can safely choose a cheaper breed or cut. Less aromatic treatments or simple plain grilling call for a better quality bird. Chicken tastes best when grilled with it's skin still on. It can of course be grilled without the skin but, because most of the fat lies just underneath, removing it will mean that the chicken will need extra oil or marinade to keep it moist and prevent drying out. Whether you are using a whole bird or joints always wash under cold running water and pat dry on kitchen paper before preparing.

Flavouring chicken and turkey

Chicken is one of the most versatile meats and makes good partnerships with so many flavours that you need never get bored with it. Adding flavour can be done in a number of ways. Marinating is one of the most popular: steep cuts or portions for about half an hour in oil or yoghurt based marinades, which can feature an endless range of spices and herbs. Dry rubs are also becoming a popular way of incorporating flavours. Chicken breasts, legs and thighs can be slashed a few times with a sharp knife to help the flavours penetrate. Butter, normally avoided because it burns, comes into it's own when grilling whole birds. Flavoured butters can be spread under the skin to seep into the breast meat as it cooks, keeping it moist while flavouring the whole bird. Even the cavity can be filled with a selection of citrus fruits, woody herbs or whole onions and garlic.

Good flavours with chicken or turkey

Tarragon ■ basil ■ mint ■ lemon balm ■ thyme ■ rosemary ■ parsley ■ yoghurt ■ paprika ■ lemon grass ■ bay leaves ■ orange ■ lemon ■ lime ■ garlic ■ ginger ■ chilli ■ cider ■ sesame oil ■ saffron ■ soy sauce ■ sherry.

Chicken on the bone: wings, drumsticks, breasts

Drumsticks and breasts require no special preparation. To prepare chicken wings, cut off and discard the small wing tips. Cut each wing at the joint to make 2 sections. Place pieces bone-side-down on the cooking grate and barbecue over Indirect Medium heat for the time given in the chart (see page 66). Always check that all chicken or turkey on the bone has been cooked thoroughly with no traces of pinkness.

Boneless chicken and turkey

Boneless chicken breasts or turkey breast meat (about 150–175g/5–6oz) can be batted out thinly (known as escalopes) and the skin removed, for making hot sandwiches. Place a piece of chicken or turkey between two sheets of greaseproof paper or cling film and bat out with a wooden rolling pin to about 1 cm/½ inch thick. Barbecue over Indirect Medium heat, according to the recipe.

Preparing a whole chicken or turkey for grilling

Twist the wing tips back under the bird. Pull the skin over the neck and cavity and secure with small metal skewer. Bring the legs together and tie with cotton string. Rub with a little olive oil, or use flavoured butters or marinades and herbs or spices.

Spatchcocking a whole chicken or poussin for grilling

Using a poultry shears or strong kitchen knife, cut along either side of the backbone and remove completely. Open out the chicken and flatten by pressing down on the breastbone with the palm of your hand. Insert a long metal skewer through the ball and socket joint of one leg and diagonally through the bird, coming out through the middle of the wing joint on the other side. Repeat with a second skewer diagonally through the leg and wing criss-crossing the first skewer.

Jointing a whole bird

Advantages to jointing a whole bird yourself is that it costs a lot less than buying individual portions and you are left with a carcass with which to make great home-made stock.

1 With the whole chicken breast side up, insert a knife between the thigh and carcass. Angle the knife inwards and cut through the ball and socket joint and remove the leg completely. Repeat with the other leg.

2 Using poultry shears or strong kitchen scissors, cut along the breastbone between the two breast sections. Cut around each breast section and remove with the wings still attached. Snip the tips off the wings.

3 Cut each breast section in half, leaving one piece with the wing attached, and cut the legs into thighs and drumsticks. You should now have 8 pieces in all – 2 drumsticks, 2 thighs, 2 breast pieces with wings and 2 breast pieces without.

Poultry kebabs

Chicken and turkey are popular candidates for grilling kebab style as they are lean and cook through quickly. Cut or dice into bite size pieces, usually about 2.5 cm/1 inch square, or cut into strips which can be threaded onto the skewer in a concertina fashion. This is popular for satay skewers.

Preparing and grilling duck or goose

When grilling a whole duck or goose you must prick the skin all over to allow the fat to escape, and always barbecue duck breasts skin side down. This should be done a few times during the cooking. If grilling duck portions over Direct heat it's very important to trim off as much fat around the edges as possible to avoid flare-ups.

Game birds: pheasant, woodcock, grouse

All game birds can be cooked on the grill, but because of their unique strong flavour, they are best grilled plain. Some birds may need to be wrapped in a few slices of streaky bacon first, as game birds can be very dry and need extra fat to moisten them.

Safety points

■ Always keep raw or cooked poultry refrigerated when not using, keeping them well separated.

■ Always thaw chicken in the refrigerator in warm weather.

■ Thoroughly wash your hands, utensils, chopping boards and work surfaces after preparing raw poultry.

■ Never use the same chopping boards, utensils or dishes for raw and cooked poultry.

■ Always cook chicken well. To test that it's cooked through, either use a food thermometer to check the internal temperature, or insert a knife into the thickest part of the piece such as the thigh. Juices should run clear with no traces of blood.

cook's guide to poultry

Whole birds and poultry pieces

Cook pieces bone side down for given time or until no longer pink in the centre. Cook whole birds breast side up. Chicken pieces with the skin on should be cooked skin side up to allow the juices to penetrate the meat. The skin can then be removed before serving for a leaner finished dish. If you plan to serve the pieces with the skin on, you can quickly sear skin side down for about 2 minutes, then turn over and finish grilling skin side up. The exception to the rule is duck breasts, which should be grilled skin side down to stop the fat running into the meat.

Type of poultry to be grilled	Weight	Cooking time	Internal temp.
Whole chicken	1.5–1.75kg/3½–4lb	1–1½ hours	180F/82C
Chicken halves (bone-in)	675–800g/1½–1¾lb	1–1¼ hours	180F/82C
Chicken breast halves (bone-in)	225g/8oz	30–35 minutes	180F/82C
Chicken breast halves (boneless)	115–175g/4–6oz	10–12 minutes	180F/82C
Chicken drumsticks/thighs (bone-in)	115–175g/4–6oz	35–45 minutes	180F/82C
Chicken wings	75 g/3oz	30 minutes	180F/82C
Whole poussin	350g–450g/12oz–1lb	45–60 minutes	180F/82C
Whole turkey (unstuffed)	5.5–7kg/10–12lb	2–3 hours	180F/82C
(General guideline: 11–13 minutes per lb)	7.25–12.5 kg/14–18lb	3–4 hours	180F/82C
Turkey breast (bone-in)	1.5 kg/3–3½lb	1–1½ hours	180F/82C
Turkey drumstick/thighs (bone-in)	450–675g/1–1½lb	¾–1¼ hours	180F/82C
Whole duck	1.75kg/4–6lb	1½–2 hours	180F/82C
Duck breasts (boneless)	approx. 225g/8oz	11–15 minutes	180F/82C
Whole pheasant	900g–1.2kg/2–2½lb	40–45 minutes	180F/82C
Whole goose	5.5–7kg/10–12lb	3 hours	180F/82C

Right: **Whole turkey grilled using the Indirect method will produce a succulent, amber-coloured turkey without basting.**

Boneless chicken and turkey

Place the chicken or turkey pieces on the cooking grate and grill over Indirect heat on a charcoal grill; set your gas grill up for Indirect Medium heat. All grilling times are based on medium-well done (the meat should no longer be pink in the centre and the juices should run clear).

Type of poultry to be grilled	Weight	Cooking time	Internal temp.
Chicken breasts	115–150g/4–6oz	10–12 minutes	170F/77C
Chicken kebabs	2.5cm/1 inch dice	10–12 minutes	170F/77C
Chicken burgers	1.5cm/¾ inch thick	10–12 minutes	170F/77C
Turkey breast escalopes	0.5–1cm/¼–½ inch thick	5–8 minutes	170F/77C
Turkey breast cubes (kebabs)	2.5cm/1 inch dice	12–15 minutes	170F/77C
Turkey breasts	1.8kg/4lb	1 hour	170F/77C

When selecting fresh ginger, choose a piece with flaky skin, as this indicates the root's freshness.

Spicy Chicken Pieces
Tandoori-style

Gas	Indirect/Medium heat	
Charcoal	Indirect	
Prep time	15 minutes + 8 hours marinating	
Grilling time	1 hour 10 minutes	Serves 6

500g/1½ pints natural yoghurt
2.5cm/1inch piece of fresh ginger, grated
3 garlic cloves, crushed
2 teaspoons paprika
2 teaspoons salt
1½ teaspoon ground cinnamon
1 teaspoon ground cumin
1 teaspoon ground coriander
Freshly ground black pepper, to taste
¼ teaspoon ground cloves
1.5kg/3–3½lb chicken pieces with skin on
Oil, for brushing
Wedges of lime to serve

1 Put the yoghurt into a large bowl. Stir in the ginger, garlic, paprika, salt, cinnamon, cumin, coriander, pepper and cloves and mix well. Set aside.

2 Using a sharp knife, make two or three deep cuts in the chicken pieces. Add the chicken to the marinade and work the marinade into the cuts. Cover and leave to marinate in the fridge for at least 8 hours.

3 Lightly brush the cooking grate with oil. Scraping off most of the marinade from the chicken pieces, barbecue over Indirect Medium heat for 1 hour–1 hour 10 minutes, turning once, until tender. Season and serve hot with wedges of lime and warm Naan bread.

Turkey Escalopes
with mustard & caramelised onions

Gas	Direct/Medium heat	☀
Charcoal	Direct	
Prep time	30 minutes	
Grilling time	10 minutes	Serves 4

6 tablespoons olive oil
2 red onions, finely sliced
1 teaspoon sugar
50 ml/2fl oz dry white wine
3½ tablespoons Dijon mustard
1 garlic clove, crushed
Salt and freshly ground black pepper
2 tablespoons mayonnaise
4 turkey escalopes
1 ciabatta loaf
A handful of rocket leaves

1 Heat 2 tablespoons oil in a saucepan, add the sliced onions and sugar and cook very gently for 15 minutes until very soft and lightly golden. Add the white wine and bring to the boil until reduced. Put aside to cool.

2 In a small bowl mix the remaining olive oil with 1½ tablespoons mustard, and the crushed garlic clove and season well. Brush over the turkey escalopes and leave aside. Mix the remaining mustard with the mayonnaise and reserve.

3 Cut the ciabatta in half lengthways, then cut each half into two pieces and put them to the side.

3 Barbecue the turkey escalopes over Direct Medium heat for 4–5 minutes. Turn over and brush with the remaining mustard oil and cook for a further 2–3 minutes until tender.

4 Toast the ciabatta pieces on the grill, cut side down, for 1–2 minutes. Spread each piece of toasted ciabatta with mustard mayonnaise. Top with a turkey escalope. Spoon the caramelised onions on the escalopes and arrange a few rocket leaves on top.

Cook's note

If you can't buy ready made turkey escalopes it's simple to make your own. You will need 150g/5oz turkey breast meat per person. Put each piece between two sheets of cling film and, using a rolling pin, bat out to about 0.5 cm/¼ inch thickness.

Above: **Turkey escalopes.**

Red onions, caramalised to bring out their rich sweet flavour, perfectly complement the turkey escalopes.

Whole Turkey
stuffed with thyme & orange

Gas	Indirect/Medium heat	✳ ✳ ✳
Charcoal	Indirect	
Prep time	30 minutes	
Grilling time	2½–3 hours	Serves 10–12

1 teaspoon coriander seeds
225g/8oz butter, softened
2 large oranges
A large bunch thyme
4.5–5.5kg/10–12lb oven ready turkey
3 bay leaves
2 tablespoons olive oil
Salt and freshly ground black pepper

1 Put the coriander seeds into a pestle and mortar and crush into a fine powder. Dry fry in a small frying pan for 1–2 minutes until it smells aromatic. Leave to cool.

2 Put the softened butter into a bowl and beat in the crushed roasted coriander. Grate the rind of the oranges and add to the butter, reserving the oranges. Add 2 tablespoons of fresh thyme leaves and beat the butter mixture until smooth. Put aside.

3 Starting at the neck end of the turkey, loosen the skin on the breast and legs, by easing your fingers between the meat and the skin, taking care not to tear the skin. Ease the butter under the skin all over the breast and legs until all the butter is used up.

4 Halve the reserved oranges and put into the cavity with the bay leaves and stalks from the thyme leaves. Tie the legs together and brush the turkey all over with olive oil and season well.

5 Put the turkey on the cooking grate and barbecue over Indirect Medium heat for 2½–3 hours (26 minutes per kg/11-13 minutes per lb) or until a skewer, inserted into the thickest part of the thigh, releases juices that run clear. The internal temperature in the meaty part of the thigh should be 170°F/77°C.

6 Transfer turkey to a platter and leave to stand for 20 minutes before carving.

Whole turkey
See picture
on page 67

Chicken Fajita Skewers
with guacamole salsa

Gas	Indirect/Medium heat	✳ ✳
Charcoal	Indirect	
Prep time	35 minutes + 30 mins marinating	
Grilling time	12–14 minutes	Serves 4

3 tablespoons olive oil
1 garlic clove, crushed
½ teaspoon ground cumin
½ teaspoon ground coriander
1 teaspoon chilli powder
Salt and freshly ground black pepper
4 boneless, skinless chicken breasts
1 red pepper
1 green pepper
1 onion

Guacamole salsa
2 ripe but firm avocados
1 lime, juice only
1 large red chilli, deseeded and finely chopped
6 spring onions, finely chopped
3 tomatoes, peeled, deseeded and diced
3 tablespoons fresh coriander, chopped

1 Put the olive oil, garlic clove, cumin, ground coriander, chilli powder and seasoning into a bowl and mix well. Cut the chicken into bite size pieces and add to the marinade. Mix well and leave for 30 minutes at room temperature. Meanwhile soak eight bamboo skewers in cold water for 30 minutes.

2 Halve and deseed the peppers. Cut each half into even bite size pieces and put aside. Cut the onion into eight wedges and leave aside.

3 Alternately thread pieces of chicken, red and green pepper and onion wedges onto the skewers. Brush any marinade remaining in the bowl onto the peppers and onion pieces.

4 Barbecue over Indirect Medium heat for 12–14 minutes, until tender.

5 Meanwhile, to make the **guacamole salsa**, halve, stone and peel the avocados. Cut the flesh into neat dice, put into a bowl and add the lime juice, red chilli, spring onion, tomato and coriander, tossing well so that the avocado is coated in the lime juice.

6 Serve the hot skewers with guacamole salsa.

Chicken fajita skewers
See picture at top left
on page 62

Make sure to brush the coriander and peppercorn mixture well between the leg and wing joints, so they flavour the whole bird.

Aromatic Chicken
with lemon balm or mint

Gas	Indirect/Medium heat	✳ ✳
Charcoal	Indirect	
Prep time	20 minutes	
Grilling time	1¼ hours	Serves 4

1 lemon
50g/2oz caster sugar
1.5 kg/3–3½lb corn-fed chicken
Bunch of lemon balm or mint
1 teaspoon black peppercorns
1 teaspoon coriander seeds
2 tablespoons olive oil
½ teaspoon salt

1 Thinly slice the lemon. Bring a saucepan of water to the boil, add the lemon slices and cook for 2 minutes. Drain and refresh the blanched lemon slices under cold running water. Put the sugar and 150 ml/¼ pint water into a clean saucepan and bring to the boil. Add the blanched lemon slices and simmer for 10 minutes. Remove from heat and leave aside to cool.

2 Meanwhile, to prepare the chicken, work your fingers between the skin and the breast meat to loosen it and then loosen the skin on the legs. Drain the lemon slices. Work the lemon slices and lemon balm or mint up under the loosened skin, over the legs and breast meat.

3 Put the peppercorns and coriander seeds into a pestle and mortar and grind coarsely. Mix with the oil and brush all over the chicken. Place the chicken on the cooking grate and barbecue over Indirect Medium heat for 1–1¼ hours until the juices run clear and the internal temperature is 170°F/77°F. Leave the chicken to rest for 10–15 minutes before carving.

Grilled Chicken Breasts
with three Chinese sauces

Gas	Direct/Medium heat	✳
Charcoal	Direct	
Prep time	25 minutes + 30 mins marinating	
Grilling time	10–12 minutes	Serves 4

1 shallot, finely chopped
1 garlic clove, crushed
4 tablespoons olive oil
4 boneless, skinless chicken breasts

Ginger soy sauce
1 teaspoon fresh ginger, grated
4 tablespoons dark soy sauce
1 tablespoon sunflower oil
Pinch of caster sugar

Spring onion sauce
1 garlic clove, crushed
4 spring onions, finely chopped
3 tablespoons sunflower oil
1 teaspoon fresh ginger, grated
3 tablespoons light soy sauce
1 tablespoon dry sherry
1 teaspoon sesame oil

Chilli sauce
3 tablespoons rice wine vinegar
½ teaspoon caster sugar
1 birds eye chilli, sliced

Szechuan peppercorns, crushed, to serve
Sea salt flakes, to serve

Clockwise from Top: **Spring onion sauce, Chilli sauce, Szechuan peppercorns, sea salt flakes, Ginger soy sauce.**

1 Put the shallot, a garlic clove and the olive oil into a bowl and mix well. Brush over the chicken breasts and leave to marinate, covered, at room temperature for 30 minutes.

2 Meanwhile, prepare the three dipping sauces. To make the **ginger soy sauce**, strain the fresh ginger into a bowl. Add the dark soy sauce, sunflower oil and caster sugar and mix together. Leave aside.

3 To make the **spring onion sauce**, mix the garlic clove, spring onions and grated ginger in a bowl. Heat the sunflower oil in a small pan until smoking hot. Pour this over the spring onion mix-ture. Add the light soy sauce, sherry and sesame oil, mix well and put aside.

4 To make the **chilli sauce**, mix the rice wine vinegar, caster sugar and chilli together and reserve.

5 Scrape the marinade off the chicken breasts and barbecue over Direct Medium heat for 10–12 minutes turning once during grilling time.

6 Put the three dipping sauces, Szechuan peppercorns and sea salt into separate shallow dishes and place in the centre of the table. Slice the grilled chicken breasts on the diagonal and serve warm with the dipping sauces.

Chicken Burgers
with blue cheese mayonnaise

Gas	Direct/Medium heat	❋ ❋
Charcoal	Direct	
Prep time	30 minutes plus chilling	
Grilling time	15 minutes	Serves 4

500g/1¼lb boneless skinless chicken thighs, or
   450g/lb chopped chicken meat
6 rashers streaky bacon, rind removed
1 tablespoon olive oil
1 garlic clove, crushed
1 shallot, finely chopped
2 tablespoons roughly chopped fresh tarragon
50g/2oz fresh white breadcrumbs

Blue cheese mayonnaise
1 egg yolk
1 teaspoon Dijon mustard
150ml/¼ pint light olive oil
1 teaspoon white wine vinegar
75g/3oz blue cheese
1 tablespoon fresh chives, chopped
4 burger buns

1 Cut the chicken thighs into pieces and put into a food processor. Cut two rashers of bacon into pieces and add to the chicken; blend until coarsely chopped. Heat the olive oil in a frying pan and add the garlic and shallot. Cook for 1–2 minutes until softened. Remove from pan, cool, and drain off excess oil.

2 Add the garlic and shallot and then the tarragon and bread-crumbs to the chicken mixture. Season and mix well. Divide into four parts. Lightly flour your hands to prevent mixture sticking then shape each part into a burger. Chill for 30 minutes.

3 For the **blue cheese mayonnaise,** whisk the egg yolk, mustard and plenty of seasoning in a bowl until smooth. Slowly whisk in the olive oil until the mixture is thick and smooth. Whisk in the vinegar. Crumble the blue cheese and fold into the mayonnaise. Add the chopped chives, and set aside to chill.

4 Grill the bacon for 8–10 minutes until crisp. Put aside. Brush the cooking grate with oil and barbecue the burgers over Direct Medium heat for 15 minutes, turning once, until tender.

5 Toast the burger buns on the grill. Arrange salad leaves on one half of the bun. Top each with a chicken burger, a spoonful of mayonnaise and a bacon rasher. Top with the other half of the bun.

Stuffed Chicken Legs
with grilled red peppers

Gas	Indirect/Medium heat	☀
Charcoal	Indirect	
Prep time	15 minutes	
Grilling time	35–45 minutes	Serves 4

20g/¾oz fresh coriander
25g/1oz fresh basil
40g/1½oz freshly grated Parmesan cheese
4 whole chicken legs
4 red peppers
Salt and pepper

1 Put the coriander, basil and Parmesan cheese into a food processor and blend until finely chopped.

2 Cut off any excess fat from the chicken legs. Work your fingers under the skin to loosen it from the flesh of the thigh and drumstick. Divide the coriander and basil mixture between the chicken legs and work it up under the skin, distributing the mixture evenly. Season the chicken well.

3 Put the chicken legs and the red peppers on the cooking grate and barbecue over Indirect Medium heat for 20 minutes turning the peppers once during cooking time.

4 Remove the peppers from the heat.Turn the chicken legs and continue cooking for a further 20–25 minutes until tender and the juices run clear.

5 Meanwhile, remove the skin, stems and seeds from the red peppers, reserving any juice that comes out of them. Remove the chicken from the grill and allow to rest for 5 minutes. Drizzle with the juice and serve warm with the grilled peppers.

Skewering the poussin keeps them in shape while they marinade and cook on the grill. Make sure to brush the poussin quickly with the apple glaze, to avoid losing any heat from the barbecue.

Spatchcocked Poussin
with apple glaze

Gas	Indirect/Medium heat	✳ ✳
Charcoal	Indirect	
Prep time	15 minutes	
Grilling time	45 minutes	Serves 4

4 poussins

Appe glaze
150ml/¼ pint pure apple juice
55g/2oz muscovado sugar
1 tablespoon cider vinegar
2 tablespoons tomato ketchup
1 orange, grated rind only
Salt and freshly ground black pepper
8 bamboo skewers, soaked in cold water

1 Soak eight bamboo skewers in cold water for 30 minutes. Using poultry shears or large kitchen scissors cut along either side of the backbone on each poussin and remove the bone. Open out the birds and press down on the breastbone to flatten out. Pin each bird into shape by pushing a skewer through one leg to come out diagonally through the wing on the other side. Crisscross with a second skewer through the other leg and opposite wing. Repeat for all four birds.

2 For the **apple glaze** put the apple juice, sugar and vinegar into a small saucepan, bring to the boil and reduce by half. Stir in the ketchup, orange rind and seasoning and mix well.

3 Put the poussins into a shallow dish and pour over the glaze. Brush well into each bird. Lift out poussins and let excess glaze run off.

4 Brush the cooking grate with a little oil. Barbecue the poussins over Indirect Medium heat for 45–50 minutes. Brush quickly with remaining glaze every 15 minutes during grilling time. Poussins are done when juices run clear, and internal temperature in the thick part of the thigh reaches 170°F/77°C. Serve with Waldorf salad (see page 139).

Orange Duck Breasts
with red wine sauce

Gas	Direct/Low heat	☀ ☀
Charcoal	Direct	
Prep time	15 minutes + 1 hour marinating	
Grilling time	15 minutes	Serves 4

4 boneless duck breasts
1 large orange, grated rind and juice
1 garlic clove, crushed
1 shallot, finely chopped
1 bay leaf
240ml/8fl oz red wine
2 tablespoons balsamic vinegar
1 teaspoon sugar
Salt and freshly ground black pepper
3 tablespoons redcurrant jelly

1 Using a sharp knife, cut off any excess fat or skin that over-hangs the edge of the meat (see cook's note below). Score the fat in a diamond pattern cutting right through to the flesh. Put into a large shallow dish in a single layer and rub the grated orange rind into the scored fat. Scatter over the garlic and shallot, add a bay leaf and pour over orange juice and red wine. Leave to marinate for at least 1 hour.

2 Remove the duck breasts from the marinade and drain well, pouring the remaining marinade into a small saucepan. Add the balsamic vinegar and sugar to the pan and bring to the boil, then simmer until reduced by half. Strain into a clean saucepan, season and whisk in the redcurrant jelly and cook for a further 1–2 minutes until slightly thickened.

3 Meanwhile, put the duck breasts skin side down on the cooking grate and barbecue over Direct Low heat for 7–8 minutes until skin is golden brown. Turn over and cook for a further 6–7 minutes until they are just firm to the touch, for medium doneness (add another 3–4 minutes cooking time for well done). Slice the duck breasts and serve with the warm sauce.

Cook's note

Duck skin has a very high fat content so it's important to trim off the excess to avoid flare-ups. If it does flare-up during cooking move away from direct heat for a minute to let the flames subside then continue cooking.

Duck Breasts
with Indonesian marinade

Gas	Indirect/Medium heat	☀ ☀
Charcoal	Indirect	
Prep time	10 minutes + 24 hours marinating	
Grilling time	10 minutes	Serves 4

4 boneless duck breasts
4 tablespoons soy sauce
2 tablespoons honey
1 tablespoon sesame seeds, toasted
3 garlic cloves, crushed
50ml/2fl oz chicken stock
1 teaspoon hoisin sauce
1½ teaspoons cornflour
1 tablespoon Sake (Japanese rice wine)
2 spring onions, finely chopped
Rice or noodles, to serve

1 Using a sharp knife trim the skin of the duck breast to about 3mm/⅛ inch and cut off any excess fat or skin that overhangs the edge of the meat. Score the remaining fat in a diamond pattern, cutting the fat right through to the flesh. This helps the excess fat to drain away. Set aside.

2 Mix together the soy sauce, honey, sesame seeds and garlic to make a marinade. Put the duck breasts into a large shallow dish in a single layer and pour over the marinade, turning the meat to coat. Cover and refrigerate for 24 hours turning occasionally.

3 Remove meat from marinade, reserving the marinade, and place in the centre of the cooking grate, skin side down. Barbecue over Indirect Medium heat for 10 minutes, turning once, then remove from the grill and leave to rest for 5 minutes.

4 Meanwhile, put the chicken stock, hoisin sauce and reserved marinade into a small saucepan, bring to the boil and simmer gently. In a small bowl, whisk together the cornflour and sake until smooth. Whisk into the saucepan and continue simmering until thickened (about 1–2 minutes).

5 Slice the duck breasts diagonally and spoon over the sauce. Sprinkle with the spring onions and serve with rice or noodles.

Crispy Duck
with pear & kumquat chutney

Gas	Indirect/Medium heat	☀ ☀
Charcoal	Indirect	
Prep time	15 minutes	
Grilling time	2 hours	Serves 4

Pear and kumquat chutney
1 tablespoon olive oil
2 firm ripe pears
8 kumquats
1 onion, roughly chopped
1 cinnamon stick
A few sprigs thyme
1 bay leaf

1.75kg/4–4½ lb oven ready duck
1 tablespoon sea salt
Salt and freshly ground black pepper

1 For the **pear and kumquat chutney**, peel and core the pears. Cut them roughly into bite-size pieces and put into a bowl. Cut the kumquats in half and add to the pears.

2 Heat the oil in a pan. Add the chopped onion and cinnamon stick. Cook for 4–5 minutes until softened. Increase the heat and add the pear, kumquats, thyme and bay leaf. Cook for a further 2–3 minutes. Remove from the heat and leave to cool.

3 Remove any giblets from the duck. Trim off the excess fat from around the cavity. Spoon in the pear and kumquat mixture.

4 Pierce the duck breast and legs several times with a skewer and sprinkle with sea salt. Place the duck on the cooking grate and barbecue over Indirect Medium heat for 2 hours, piercing the duck skin every 30 minutes to let excess fat escape. The duck is cooked when the juices run clear. Leave to rest for 15 minutes before cutting.

5 Spoon the pear and kumquat chutney from the duck cavity into a serving bowl, removing the thyme sprigs and bay leaf. Season well and serve warm with the duck.

Cook's note

Taste the chutney stuffing before you serve it and if it's a little sharp add a good pinch of sugar. The taste will depend upon how sweet the pears are and how sharp the kumquats are.

meat

Some of the best 'come and get it' aromas in the world are the rich, sweet, charred smells of meat grilling on a barbecue. Traditionally sausages, burgers and steaks have been the long-time favourites. Extending that repertoire to include joints such as rack of lamb, pork tenderloin and even whole glazed ham will result in an impressive range of tasty meals that are easy to cook on the barbecue.

Delicious recipes include orange apricot glazed ham, char-sui pork with plum sauce and, using the more traditional ingredients with a mouthwatering twist, pepper-crushed sirloin steaks and Bratwurst sausages with red cabbage sauerkraut.

perfect meat

When buying beef or lamb for grilling, look for meat with a good marbling of fat (tiny veins of fat running through the meat). Fat gives meat it's flavour but as you will be trimming off most of the outer fat to avoid flare-ups, it is important to have good marbling.

Beef should have a bright red flesh while lamb has a dull red appearance. Pork and veal both have a pale pink flesh with no marbling. The fat of pork should be smooth and white while veal fat is pinkish white.

If possible buy your steaks from a butcher where you can ask for them to be cut to a certain thickness which will allow the grilling guides to be followed as closely as possible.

Safety points

- Always keep raw or cooked meat refrigerated when not using and never store them near each other.

- Always thaw meat in the refrigerator.

- Thoroughly wash your hands, utensils, chopping boards and work surfaces after preparing raw meat.

- Never use the same chopping boards, utensils or dishes for raw and cooked meat dishes.

Right: **Lamb cutlets held in a meat shape with soaked cocktail sticks are simply grilled with oil and fresh rosemary.**

Opposite: **A meat thermometer is invaluable when grilling meat thicker than one inch. Insert into the centre of the thickest part of the meat near the end of the cooking time given in the recipe.**

Flavouring meat

Beef, lamb, pork and veal can all be flavoured in a variety of ways. Spice rubs are a good method as the toughness of raw meat stands up well to the pressure needed to apply them. Marinating is also good as long as the meat is in the marinade for at least 1 hour. You can make a few slashes in the meat before applying the marinade or spice rub. Sauces or glazes should, as usual, be brushed on shortly before the end of grilling time.

Good flavours for beef

Onions ■ paprika ■ cinnamon ■ ginger ■ cardamom ■ peppercorns ■ garlic ■ brandy ■ port ■ yoghurt ■ parsley ■ horseradish ■ mustard ■ soy sauce ■ chillies.

Good flavours for lamb

Garlic ■ rosemary ■ mint ■ lemon ■ yoghurt ■ chillies.

Good flavours for pork and veal

Garlic ■ chillies ■ star anise ■ soy sauce ■ maple syrup ■ sesame oil ■ ginger ■ rosemary ■ sage ■ thyme ■ apple ■ mustard ■ honey.

Large cuts of meat

Larger cuts, such as brisket of beef, pork roast or a leg of lamb, should be grilled over Direct heat. A leg of lamb can also be boned and cooked flat. For any roasts that contain a lot of fat it's advisable to place them on a roasting rack set inside a heavy-duty foil tray. If the fat in the tray begins to burn add a little water to it.

Steaks, chops and other small cuts

Steaks are one of the most popular cuts of meat for barbecues. Brush the meat or the cooking grate with a little oil before grilling any meats unless they have been marinated in an oily marinade. Our cooking guide gives you approximate times for grilling steaks to medium, but with experience you will be able to judge cooking times exactly and grill meat to your own liking.

Searing meat on the barbecue

Searing meat is no different on the barbecue than searing it in a frying pan. It helps keep the meat moist by sealing in most of the juices before you complete the rest of the cooking. Also, the hot fat drips from the meat as it sears, creating the smoke that gives barbecued food its distinctive flavour. To sear meat on a gas grill, preheat it to High, then place the meat over Direct heat and shut the lid on the grill. Cook for about 2 minutes for any cut of meat up to 2.5cm/1 inch and 3-4 minutes for anything thicker. (Remember to trim any excess fat from the meat. If there is flaring, turn off the centre burner until the flaring subsides, then turn it back onto to Low or Medium.) Once seared, complete cooking by the Indirect method over Medium heat, following the recipe directions. To sear meat on a charcoal grill follow the same procedure as outlined above. Place the meat directly over the coals with the lid closed to sear, then finish cooking over Indirect heat. If you have set up a charcoal barbecue for the Indirect method, ie: where the coals are arranged at either side of the kettle, simply sear the meat over the coals near the edge of the grill, then move it to the middle of the cooking grate to finish Indirectly. If you have the grill set up for Direct cooking, after searing the meat move it to the outside of the cooking grate for finishing, away from the direct heat source. This combined grilling method is ideal for thicker steaks and chops and small roasts.

Meat kebabs

Beef, lamb, pork and veal can all be given the kebab treatment. Remember, if a cut of meat requires long or slow cooking, it won't be suitable for kebabs. Choose tender cuts of meat that can be cooked within 25 minutes. Trim off any excess fat and cut into bite size pieces usually about 2.5 cm/1 inch square. Metal and bamboo skewers are suitable for meat kebabs, and woody rosemary stalks make good skewers and add great flavour, particularly with lamb. Soak these and wooden skewers for 30 minutes.

cook's guide to meat

With the exception of burgers, cooking meat on a barbecue or grill is the subject most outdoor cooks feel somewhat uneasy about. With the following guidelines and charts you can learn how to cook a piece of meat no matter what the cut or thickness, but your eye will become your true guide in time. With experience, you will be able to tell exactly at what point to remove the meat from the grill, whether your taste is for rare or well done. If you are unsure whether a piece of meat is cooked through, simply take it off the grill and place on a clean board. Insert a knife into the centre of the meat and if the juices run clear with no traces of blood, this indicates the meat is cooked through. If the juices are bloody, return the meat to the grill.

Beef & Veal

All times are based on medium (cook a little longer for well done); turn meat once halfway through cooking. Always let the meat rest, covered with aluminium foil, for 10–15 minutes after removing from the grill. This not only allows the juices to settle for full flavour, but the meat continues cooking during this time and the internal temperature rises to a perfect medium finish. You can cover the meat with aluminium foil to keep it warm. Steaks should be grilled using the Direct method. For roasts or large cuts of meat, grill using the Indirect method for the time given.

Type of beef to be grilled	Weight	Cooking time	Internal temp.
Sirloin fillet, T-bone or rib steak	2.5cm/1 inch thick	8–10 minutes	160F/71C
	4cm/1½ inches thick	14–16 minutes	160F/71C
	5cm/2 inches thick	15–20 minutes	160F/71C
Thick rump tip or rump steak	450–900g/1–2lb	7 minutes each side	160F/71C
Brisket	2.25–2.75kg/5–6lb	2½ –3 hours	160F/71C
Boneless sirloin roast	1.75–2.75kg/4–6lb	2–2½ hours	160F/71C
Hamburger	2cm/¾ inch thick	approx. 10 minutes	160F/71C
Veal chops	2cm/¾ inch thick	10–12 minutes	160F/71C
	2.5cm/1 inch thick	14 minutes	160F/71C
	3.5cm/1½ inches thick	16–18 minutes	160F/71C

Lamb

Grill lamb chops using the Direct method. All times are based on medium (cook a little longer for well done); turn meat once halfway through cooking. Let the meat rest, covered with aluminium foil, for 10–15 minutes after removing from the grill. The meat continues cooking during this time and the internal temperature rises to a perfect medium finish. For roasts or large cuts of meat, grill using the Indirect method for the time given.

Type of lamb to be grilled	Weight	Cooking time	Internal temp.
Loin, rib and chump chops	2.5cm/1 inch thick	10–12 minutes	160F/71C
	5cm/2 inches thick	14–16 minutes	160F/71C
Leg steaks	2.5cm/1 inch	10–12 minutes	160F/71C
Leg of lamb, boneless/butterflied	1.75kg/4lb	55–65 minutes	160F/71C
Leg of lamb, boneless and rolled	2.25–2.75kg/6½lb	1½–2 hours	160F/71C
Rib crown roast	1.5–1.75kg/3–4lb	1¼–1½ hours	160F/71C
Rib roast	1.2–1.5kg/2½–3lb	1¼–1½ hours	160F/71C

Pork

Grill pork chops using the Direct method when 2–2.5cm/¾–1 inch in thickness and the Indirect method/Medium heat for thicker chops. All times are based on medium-well done (pork should no longer be pink in the centre). Turn meat once halfway during grilling time. Let the meat rest, covered with aluminium foil, for 10–15 minutes after removing from the grill. The meat continues cooking during this time and the internal temperature rises to a perfect medium finish. For pork roasts, follow the same method as for beef or lamb. Sausages should be cooked using the Direct method, being careful of flare-ups if they are especially fatty. As with all pork they should be cooked well and no longer pink in the centre.

Type of pork to be grilled	Weight	Cooking time	Internal temp.
Rib, loin and shoulder chops	2cm/¾–1 inch thick	12–14 minutes	160F/71C
Loin roast	1.5–2.25kg/3–5lb	1¾ hours	160F/71C
Spare ribs	1.5–1.75/3–4lb	1–1½ hours	160F/71C
Tenderloin (pork steaks)	350–450g/¾–1lb	25–35 minutes	160F/71C
Sausages	thick/large	25 minutes	160F/71C

Provençal Rack of Lamb
with white bean salad

Gas	Direct/Medium heat	✳ ✳ ✳
Charcoal	Direct	
Prep time	15 minutes + 4–6 hrs marinating	
Grilling time	15–25 minutes	Serves 4

1 small onion, roughly chopped

6 garlic cloves, roughly chopped

4 plum tomatoes, roughly chopped

15 g/½oz fresh rosemary sprigs

15 g/½oz fresh parsley

2 tablespoons Dijon mustard

300 ml/½ pint red wine

1 teaspoon sea salt

½ teaspoon freshly ground black pepper

2 racks of lamb, about 675g/1½lb in weight, French trimmed

White bean salad

250g/9oz dried cannellini beans

900ml/1½ pints chicken stock

1 small onion, quartered

1 carrot, cut into four

1 celery stalk, cut into four

1½ teaspoons dried oregano

50ml/2fl oz extra virgin olive oil

1 tablespoon red wine vinegar

2 tablespoons fresh parsley, chopped

2 large tomatoes, diced

50g/2oz black or green olives, sliced

Salt and freshly ground black pepper

Bone burns and blackens quite easily so it is important to cover any bones with foil before grilling.

1 Put the onion, garlic, tomatoes, rosemary, parsley, mustard and red wine into a food processor, season and blend to a purée. Pour into a large non-metallic bowl. Trim excess fat from the lamb and add to the marinade; coat evenly, then cover and chill for 4–6 hours.

2 For the **white bean salad**, put the dried beans into a large saucepan and cover with at least twice their volume of water. Bring to the boil and simmer for 10 minutes; remove from the heat and soak for 1 hour. Drain and rinse. Return the beans to the saucepan with the stock, onion, carrot, celery and oregano. Bring to the boil, reduce heat and simmer for 1–1½ hours until tender. Discard the vegetables, drain the beans and transfer to a serving bowl. Add the olive oil, vinegar, parsley, tomatoes and olives; season well, and leave aside to cool.

3 Remove the lamb from the marinade. Cover the bones with tin foil to prevent them from burning. Barbecue the lamb over Direct Medium heat – 15 minutes for rare, 20 minutes for Medium rare and 25 minutes for well done – turning once. Let the lamb rest for 10–15 minutes, before slicing into cutlets and serving with the white bean salad.

Bratwurst Rolls
with soused red cabbage

Gas	Indirect/Medium heat	☀
Charcoal	Indirect	
Prep time	45 minutes	
Grilling time	16–18 minutes	Serves 6

375g/12oz red cabbage
1 onion
2 tablespoons sunflower oil
2 garlic cloves, crushed
½ tablespoon caraway seeds
120ml/4fl oz cider vinegar
2 tablespoons soft brown sugar
Salt and freshly ground black pepper
6 bratwurst sausages
Oil, for brushing
6 hot dog buns, split
Hot mustard, to serve

1 Using a sharp knife or a food processor, very finely shred the red cabbage and onion. Heat the oil in a large saucepan and add the cabbage, onion and garlic and stir-fry for 5–6 minutes, until softened.

2 Add the caraway seeds and stir-fry for a further 1–2 minutes. Add the vinegar, brown sugar and seasoning, bring to the boil, then reduce heat, cover and cook for 25 minutes until very soft. Turn off heat and leave aside to cool completely.

3 Lightly brush the sausages with oil and barbecue over Indirect Medium heat for 16–18 minutes, turning once, until tender.

4 Spread each bun or roll with a little mustard, then fill with the soused red cabbage, top with a sausage and serve.

Rosemary Veal Chops
with grilled mushroom relish

Gas	Direct/Medium heat	❋ ❋
Charcoal	Direct	
Prep time	15 minutes	
Grilling time	25 minutes	Serves 4

2 tablespoons olive oil
1 tablespoons fresh rosemary, finely chopped
2 cloves garlic, finely chopped
½ lemon, grated rind only
½ teaspoon sea salt
4 veal rib chops, about 2.5cm/1 inch in thickness

Grilled mushroom relish
1 onion
225g/8oz fresh large shitake mushrooms
2 tablespoons olive oil
Salt and freshly ground black pepper
1 small red tomato, seeded and diced
1 small yellow tomato, seeded and diced
1 tablespoon chopped fresh thyme
2 teaspoons sherry vinegar
1 tablespoon extra virgin olive oil
1 tablespoon chopped fresh parsley

1 In a small bowl, mix the olive oil, rosemary, garlic, grated lemon rind and salt. Brush the mixture over both sides of the veal chops, cover and chill while you prepare the grilled mushrooms.

2 To prepare the **grilled mushroom relish**, slice the onion into thick rings and put into a bowl with the shitake mushrooms and the olive oil. Toss gently to coat and season well. Grill the mushrooms and onions over Direct Medium heat, for 10 minutes, turning once, until tender and golden. Cool and chop roughly. Transfer to a serving bowl and add the tomatoes, thyme, sherry vinegar, olive oil and parsley. Toss well and check seasoning then set aside.

3 Remove the veal chops from the marinade and grill over Direct Medium heat for 12–15 minutes, turning once. They should be slightly pink in the centre.

4 Allow the veal chops to rest for 5–10 minutes, then serve with the grilled mushroom relish.

Honey Mustard Sausages
with onion skewers

Gas	Indirect/Medium heat	
Charcoal	Indirect	☀
Prep time	10 minutes	
Grilling time	18 minutes	**Serves 6**

3 garlic cloves, crushed

1 lemon, juice only

3 tablespoons wholegrain mustard

3 tablespoons liquid honey

1 teaspoon chilli powder

2 large onions

12 large pork sausages

Oil, for brushing

1 Put the garlic, lemon juice, wholegrain mustard, honey and chilli into a bowl and mix well. Put aside.

2 Cut the onions in half, cutting through the root to keep the layers of onion intact. Cut each half into quarters. Cut each quarter into two or three wedges, keeping each intact. Skewer the wedges onto two or three long skewers.

3 Brush the sausages and the onion wedges all over with the mustard and honey mixture. Brush the sausages and onion skewers with oil and place them in the centre of the cooking grate. Barbecue over Indirect Medium heat for 6 minutes. Turn over and grill for a further 12 minutes until sausages and onion wedges are tender.

4 Put the sausages into a large serving dish. Run a fork down the skewers to remove the onion wedges. Add to the sausages, mix well and serve with hand-cut French fries (see page 106)

Grilled Steak
with tomato relish

Gas	Direct/Medium heat	
Charcoal	Direct	☀
Prep time	5 minutes	
Grilling time	12–16 minutes	**Serves 4**

4 T-bone steaks, about 225–325g/8–12oz each in weight

Salt and freshly ground black pepper

8 medium plum tomatoes, halved lengthwise

2 tablespoons olive oil

1 large onion, finely chopped

1 clove garlic, finely chopped

3 tablespoons fresh basil, shredded

1 Season steaks well and arrange on the cooking grate directly over the heat. Brush the tomatoes lightly with a little of the oil and arrange, cut side up, around the steaks. Barbecue over Direct Medium heat for 6–8 minutes, turning once until tomatoes are softened. Remove tomatoes from the grill and set aside. Turn the steaks and continue grilling for another 6–8 minutes for medium, 8–11 minutes for well done.

2 Put remaining oil, onion and garlic in a small ovenproof frying pan. Set the frying pan on the side burner and cook for 6–8 minutes, stirring the onion mixture occasionally, until onions and garlic have softened and are tinged with brown. If your grill does not have a side burner, you can place the saucepan directly on the cooked grate, being careful to keep the handle away from the heat.

3 Roughly chop the tomatoes and stir into the onion with the basil and season to taste. Remove steaks from the grill and allow to rest for 5 minutes then divide steaks between serving plates. Stir any residue meat juices into tomato relish and serve with steaks.

Grilled steak
See picture at top left
on page 84

Lamb Rib Chops
with ginger & port

Gas	Indirect/Medium heat	✹ ✹
Charcoal	Indirect	
Prep time	20 minutes	
Grilling time	7–17 minutes	Serves 4

300ml/½ pint chicken stock
50ml/2fl oz ketchup
50ml/2fl oz tomato purée
1 small onion, finely chopped
1 celery stalk, finely chopped
50ml/2fl oz port
2 tablespoons honey
1 tablespoon freshly grated ginger
1 tablespoon brown sauce
1 tablespoon balsamic vinegar
1 tablespoon Worcestershire sauce
2 teaspoons chilli powder
2 teaspoons mustard powder
2 teaspoons soft light brown sugar
8 lamb rib chops

1 Put the chicken stock, ketchup, tomato purée, onion, celery, port, honey, ginger, brown sauce, balsamic vinegar, Worcestershire sauce, chilli powder, mustard powder and brown sugar into a saucepan. Bring to the boil and simmer uncovered for 1 hour, stirring occasionally until sauce is thickened. Pour into a food processor or blender and blend until smooth. Leave to cool then chill until required. The sauce can be made up to 3 days in advance and stored in the refrigerator.

2 Barbecue the lamb chops over Indirect Medium heat, 7–9 minutes for rare, 10–13 minutes for medium rare or 14–17 minutes for well done, turning once during cooking. Brush each side with the sauce for the last 2 minutes of grilling time. Remove chops from the grill and allow rest for 3–4 minutes. Meanwhile, heat any remaining sauce and serve with the chops.

Lamb rib chops
See picture at bottom left on page 84

Lamb Kebabs
with a cognac herb sauce

Gas	Indirect/Medium heat	✹
Charcoal	Indirect	
Prep time	10 minutes	
Grilling time	7–17 minutes	Serves 4

2 green peppers, deseeded, cut into 2.5cm/1 inch pieces
675 g/1½lb boneless leg of lamb, trimmed and cut into
    2.5cm/1 inch cubes
1 large onion, cut into 8 wedges
Salt and freshly ground black pepper

Cognac herb sauce
120ml/4fl oz olive oil
1 small onion, roughly chopped
1 lemon, juice only
2 tablespoons cognac or brandy
1 garlic clove, roughly chopped
2 teaspoons Dijon mustard
1 teaspoon dried oregano
1 tablespoon chopped fresh thyme
Pinch of cayenne
Vegetable oil, for brushing

1 If using wooden skewers soak eight in cold water for 30 minutes. Thread lamb, pepper pieces and onion wedges onto the skewers. Season and set aside.

2 To prepare the **cognac herb sauce**, put the olive oil, chopped onion, lemon juice, cognac or brandy, garlic, mustard, oregano, thyme and cayenne into a food processor or blender and blend until smooth.

3 Lightly oil the kebabs and barbecue over Indirect Medium heat, 7–9 minutes for rare, 10–13 minutes for medium doneness, or 14–17 minutes for well done, turning once and brushing liberally with the sauce two or three times during cooking.

Properties in the plum stones help to thicken the sauce. Wrapped in muslin, the stones are easy to fish out, as are the hard spices.

When you remove the muslin bags, squeeze them and drain any juices back into the sauce.

Cook's note

If you can't get hold of fresh plums to make the sauce then most good Chinese grocery stores sell plum sauce in jars or bottles.

Char-sui Pork
with plum sauce

Gas	Indirect/Medium heat	✳ ✳
Charcoal	Indirect	
Prep time	50 minutes + 4 hours marinating	
Grilling time	30 minutes	Serves 6

Char-sui marinade
4 tablespoons black treacle
2 tablespoons dark soy sauce
3 tablespoons dry sherry
3 pork tenderloins, each weighing about 375–450g/12oz–1lb

Plum sauce
675g/1½lb fresh plums
10 whole cloves
1 star anise
2 small dried chillies
250g/9oz brown sugar
1 teaspoon salt
2.5cm/1 inch piece fresh ginger, finely chopped
350ml/12fl oz white wine vinegar
Oil, for brushing

1 To make the **char-sui marinade**, put the treacle, soy sauce and sherry into a small saucepan and stir over a gentle heat until well combined. Put aside to cool.

2 Trim the pork tenderloins of any excess fat and put into a large shallow dish. Pour over the cool char-sui marinade, turning the tenderloins to make sure they are completely coated in the sauce. Cover and put into the fridge to marinate for 4 hours.

3 For the **plum sauce**, cut the plums in half and remove the stones. Crack the stones with a hammer and tie in a piece of muslin. In a second piece of muslin, tie the cloves, star anise and chillies. Put the two muslin bags into a large saucepan with the plums, sugar, salt, ginger and vinegar.

4 Bring the pan slowly to the boil until the sugar has dissolved, then simmer for 20 minutes until the plums are very soft. Remove the muslin bags and squeeze them over the pan. Boil vigorously for a further 5–10 minutes until thickened. Leave to cool (the sauce will thicken more when it's cooler).

5 Brush the cooking grate with a little oil. Remove the tenderloins from the marinade and barbecue over Indirect Medium heat for 30 minutes. Slice the tenderloins and serve hot or cold with the plum sauce.

Grilled Pork Shoulder
with spicy herb rub

Gas	Indirect/Medium heat	✻
Charcoal	Indirect	
Prep time	10 minutes	
Grilling time	10 minutes	Serves 8

1½ tablespoons paprika

1 tablespoon ground coriander

1 tablespoon lemon rind, finely grated

1 tablespoon dried marjoram

2 teaspoons garlic powder

1 teaspoon salt

¾ teaspoon freshly ground pepper

½ teaspoon ground cumin

¼ teaspoon caraway seeds, crushed

¼ teaspoon ground cinnamon

8 boneless pork shoulder steaks, cut ¾–inch thick
(about 175g/6 ounces each)

1 In a small bowl combine the paprika, coriander, lemon rind, marjoram, garlic powder, salt, pepper, cumin, caraway seeds and cinnamon. Rub the herb mixture on both sides of the steaks, pressing into the surface.

2 Barbecue the steaks over Indirect Medium heat for 10 minutes for medium cooked steaks, or 12 to 14 minutes for well done. Turn the steaks once halfway through grilling time.

Cook's note

1.5–1.75kg/3–4lb of country-style spare ribs can be substituted for pork shoulder steaks. For 1.5–1.75kg/3–4lb of country-style ribs, prepare as above and barbecue over Indirect Medium heat for 1¼ to 1½ hours.

Pepper-crusted Steaks
with brandy cream sauce

Gas	Direct/High heat	✻ ✻ ✻
Charcoal	Direct	
Prep time	10 minutes	
Grilling time	8 minutes	Serves 4

3 tablespoons black peppercorns

4 sirloin steaks, about 225g/8oz each in weight

Brandy cream sauce

1 tablespoon vegetable oil

1 onion or shallot, finely chopped

1 small garlic clove, crushed

2 tablespoons brandy

300 ml/½pint good quality beef stock

6 tablespoons crème fraiche

Salt and freshly ground black pepper

Oil, for brushing

1 Put the peppercorns into a mortar and pestle and coarsely grind. Trim any excess fat from the steaks. Spill the crushed peppercorns onto a sheet of greaseproof paper and spread out. Press one side of each steak onto the peppercorns and shake off excess. Repeat with all the steaks until the peppercorns are used up.

2 To make the **brandy cream sauce**, heat the oil in a small saucepan. Add the onion (or shallot) and garlic and cook over a gentle heat for 2–3 minutes until softened, then pour in the brandy, ignite and cook until flames subside. Add the beef stock and cook for a further 10–12 minutes until reduced to about 3½fl oz/100ml. Add the crème fraiche and cook for 5 minutes until very slightly thickened. Season well and keep warm.

3 Brush the steaks with a little oil and barbecue over Direct High heat for 8 minutes, turning once, for medium doneness. For well done, add 2–3 minutes each side. Serve with the hot brandy cream sauce.

Above Left: **Grilled pork shoulder.**

Above Right: **Pepper-crusted steak.**

When turning the steak on the grill, be careful not to knock off the peppercorn coating, as this gives the steak its distinctive flavour.

Grilled Steak
with sweet Asian marinade

Gas	Direct/Medium heat	✱ ✱
Charcoal	Direct	
Prep time	5 minutes + 3–4 hrs marinating	
Grilling time	12–15 minutes	Serves 4

120ml/4fl oz soy sauce

120ml/4fl oz plum sauce

120ml/4fl oz pineapple juice

120ml/4fl oz ketchup

2 spring onions, finely chopped

3 tablespoons fresh coriander, chopped

5cm/2 inch piece fresh ginger, grated

4 garlic cloves, finely chopped

500g/1¼lb thick rump tip or rump steak

1 Put the soy sauce, plum sauce, pineapple juice, ketchup, spring onions, coriander, ginger and garlic into a small bowl and mix well. Put the steak into a large shallow dish and pour over the marinade, turning the meat to coat. Cover and chill for 3–4 hours, turning the meat occasionally.

2 Remove the steak from marinade, reserving the marinade. Barbecue the steak over Direct Medium heat, for 12–15 minutes turning once and brushing occasionally with some of the reserved marinade. Allow the steaks to rest for 5 minutes before slicing them thinly.

3 Meanwhile, put most of the reserved marinade into a small saucepan and bring to the boil. Simmer rapidly for 5 minutes until reduced by about one third and serve with the sliced steak.

Whole Roast Ham
with orange apricot glaze

Gas	Indirect/Medium heat	✱ ✱
Charcoal	Indirect	
Prep time	5 minutes	
Grilling time	1½–2 hours	Serves 8–10

1.5–2.25kg/3½–5lb cooked boneless ham joint

Whole cloves, to decorate

Orange apricot glaze

90g/3½oz apricot preserve

50ml/2fl oz orange juice

2 tablespoons soy sauce

½ lemon, juice only

1 Using a sharp knife cut off the outer skin of the ham leaving a thick layer of fat. Score the fat of the ham, making diagonal cuts about 2.5cm/1 inch apart, to give a diamond pattern. Insert a whole clove in the centre of each diamond.

2 For the **orange apricot glaze**, mix together the apricot preserve, orange juice, soy sauce and lemon juice and then set aside.

3 Barbecue the ham over Indirect Medium heat for 1½–2 hours. During the last 15 minutes of cooking time, brush the ham all over with the glaze. Remove from the grill and leave to stand for 15 minutes before cutting.

4 Just before serving, heat the remaining glaze and brush the ham all over with more glaze.

Cook's note

To cook a 1.5–2.25kg/3½–5lb boneless ham joint, put into a large saucepan of cold water and bring to the boil. Pour off the water and top up with cold water bringing to the boil again and cook for 20 minutes per 450g/1lb.

Right: **Glazed whole roast ham.**

american classics

America has enjoyed generations of barbecuing, and as a nation, has perfected a range of classic dishes that have become perennial favourites. Cooking on the barbecue is a family occasion which extends to outdoor entertaining in the backyard. Traditional and inspirational recipes share equal status at the table, and a wealth of international tastes complement the all-American classics.

'Barbecue' in the American culinary tradition means cooking meat slowly over low heat. Sample the classic recipes in this chapter which show this method at its best – a slow roasted brisket, or pulled pork barbecue.

For simple and delicious meals, the Kansas City-style pork spare ribs with a tangy BBQ sauce are a treat, or try corn on the cob with chilli and coriander. Of course, there is always the quintessential American favourite, hamburger and (yes, grilled!) French fries.

Hand-cut French Fries
with spicy ketchup

Gas	Direct/Medium heat	✳
Charcoal	Direct	
Prep time	10 minutes	
Grilling time	10–12 minutes	Serves 4

Spicy ketchup

150ml/¼ pint ketchup
1 tablespoons chilli sauce
2 teaspoons balsamic vinegar

900g/2lb potatoes, unpeeled
2 tablespoons olive oil
2 large garlic cloves, finely chopped
Salt and freshly ground black pepper

1 To make the **spicy ketchup**, put the ketchup, chilli sauce and vinegar into a small bowl, mix well and set aside.

2 Cut the potatoes in half then cut each half into four wedges or chunks. Put the olive oil, garlic and seasoning into a large bowl and mix well. Add the potato chunks and toss well until evenly coated.

3 Place the potato wedges on the grill, being careful not to let them drop through the grate. Barbecue over Direct Medium heat for 10–12 minutes, turning once, until golden brown on both sides. For extra crispness, open the lid during the last 2 minutes of grilling time. Serve hot with the spicy ketchup.

Classic Hamburgers
in toasted sesame buns

Gas	Direct/Medium heat	✳
Charcoal	Direct	
Prep time	10 minutes	
Grilling time	12–16 minutes	Serves 4

675g/1½lb lean beef mince
2 garlic cloves, crushed
½ onion, coarsely grated
1 tablespoon Worcestershire sauce
225g/8oz Cheddar cheese, thinly sliced (optional)
Salt and pepper
4 sesame hamburger buns or crusty rolls, split
Sliced onion, sliced tomato, lettuce, mayonnaise,
**   mustard, ketchup, cucumber relish to serve**

1 In a large bowl, mix together the beef mince, garlic, onion, Worcestershire sauce and plenty of seasoning. Divide the mixture into four parts and shape into burgers.

2 Barbecue over Direct Medium heat for 12–16 minutes, turning once until cooked through. For cheeseburgers, top the hamburgers with the cheese for the last 2–3 minutes of grilling time. Arrange the hamburger buns or rolls cut side down around the burgers for the last 2–3 minutes of grilling time to toast.

3 To serve, put one hamburger onto one half of each bun, add the topping of your choice, and place the remaining half bun on top.

**Classic hamburger with
hand-cut French fries.**

Hand-cut French fries
See picture at bottom left
on page 104

Buffalo-style Ribs
with blue cheese dressing

Gas	Indirect/Medium heat	☀
Charcoal	Indirect	
Prep time	10 minutes + 4 hours marinating	
Grilling time	30 –35 minutes	Serves 4

50ml/2fl oz cider vinegar
50ml/2fl oz olive oil
50ml/2fl oz Worcestershire sauce
2–3 tablespoons chilli sauce, to taste
1 tablespoon soft dark brown sugar
1.5 kg/3 –3½ lb pork back ribs, in one piece

Blue cheese dressing
50ml/2fl oz mayonnaise
50ml/2fl oz soured cream
50g/2oz blue cheese, finely crumbled
1 garlic clove, finely chopped
½ teaspoon Worcestershire sauce
1–2 tablespoons milk
Salt and freshly ground black pepper

1 Put the vinegar, olive oil, Worcestershire sauce, chilli sauce and brown sugar into a small bowl and whisk together. Put the ribs into a large non–metallic dish, pour over the marinade and turn the ribs to coat. Cover the dish with cling film and chill for at least 4 hours or overnight, turning the ribs occasionally to distribute the marinade.

2 Meanwhile, to prepare the **blue cheese dressing**, put the mayonnaise, soured cream, blue cheese, garlic, and Worcestershire sauce into a small bowl and mix well. Add a little milk if the dressing is too thick. Season and chill until required.

3 Remove the ribs from the marinade and put the marinade into a small saucepan. Bring to the boil and boil hard for 1 minute, remove and set aside.

4 Place the ribs on the cooking grate bone side down (or use a rib rack) and barbecue over Indirect Medium heat for 30–35 minutes, turning once and brushing with the boiled marinade, until tender. Allow them to sit for 5 minutes before cutting into individual ribs and serving with the blue cheese dressing.

Steak Sandwich
drizzled with Santa Maria sauce

Gas	Indirect/Medium heat	✳ ✳
Charcoal	Indirect	
Prep time	10 minutes + 24 hrs marinating	Serves 4
Grilling time	12–20 minutes	

1 tablespoon coarsely ground black pepper
2 garlic cloves, crushed
1 teaspoon mustard powder
1 teaspoon paprika
Pinch cayenne pepper
1 kg/2½lb piece rump steak or rump tip, 5cm/2 in thick

Santa Maria sauce
1 tablespoon olive oil
1 red onion, finely chopped
1 clove garlic, finely chopped
120ml/4fl oz chicken stock
4 tablespoons ketchup
4 tablespoons brown sauce
1 tablespoon fresh parsley, chopped
1 tablespoon Worcestershire sauce
1½ teaspoons ground coffee
French bread, to serve
Oak/mesquite/hickory chips soaked for 30 minutes before grilling

1 Put the black pepper, garlic, mustard, paprika and cayenne into a bowl and mix well. Rub the mixture into the surface of the meat, cover with cling film and chill for 4 hours or up to 24 hours.

2 Meanwhile, to prepare the **Santa Maria sauce**, heat the olive oil in a saucepan, add the onion and garlic and fry gently for 3–4 minutes until softened. Add the chicken stock, ketchup, brown sauce, parsley, Worcestershire sauce, ground coffee and black pepper and bring to the boil. Simmer gently, stirring occasionally, until reduced to about 300ml/10fl oz. Pour into a food processor or blender and purée. Leave to cool, cover and chill until required but allow it to return to room temperature before serving.

3 Follow the grill's instructions for using wood chips (wood smoke enhances the flavour of the steak). Sear the steak over Direct Medium heat for 5 minutes, turning once. Finish over Indirect Medium heat, 8–10 minutes for rare, 10–13 minutes for medium, and 13–15 minutes for well done, turning once. Allow the meat to sit for 5 minutes before slicing. Sandwich the sliced meat and spoonfuls of the sauce between chunks of French bread and serve warm or at room temperature.

Corn on the Cob

Gas	Indirect/Medium heat	☀
Charcoal	Indirect	
Prep time	10 minutes + soaking	
Grill time	20 minutes	Serves 4

4 ears of corn with husks still attached
115g/4oz butter, softened

1 Soak the corn in their husks in plenty of cold water for 30 minutes.

2 Remove corn and shake to get rid of excess water. Gently peel back husks without tearing the cob then remove and discard the silk. Smear the corn with butter and fold the husks back around the corn. Tie with cotton thread around the top to enclose.

3 Arrange corn on cooking grate and barbecue over Indirect Medium heat for 20–30 minutes until tender.

Corn with Jerk Sauce

2 onions, chopped
2 garlic cloves, crushed
4 tablespoons lime juice
2 tablespoons dark molasses
2 tablespoons soy sauce
2 tablespoons fresh ginger, chopped
2 jalapeno chillies, deseeded and chopped
½ teaspoon ground cinnamon
¼ teaspoon ground allspice
¼ teaspoon ground nutmeg
6 ears of corn, husks removed

Put all the ingredients into a food processor and blend until finely chopped. Put each ear of husked corn on a large sheet of foil and spoon over the jerk sauce. Wrap the foil around the corn and sauce and barbecue over Indirect Medium heat for 15–20 minutes until tender.

Corn with Chilli & Coriander

115g/4oz butter, softened
1 red chilli, deseeded and finely chopped
1 tablespoon fresh coriander, chopped

Beat together the butter, chilli and coriander, use in place of the butter and continue as for top recipe.

Make sure you don't completely pull off the husks, just peel back like a banana, then smear the butter all over with a fork or spoon.

The husks will stick to the butter when folded back, but you still need to tie them at the top, otherwise they will come undone when the butter melts.

Cook's note

If the corn has insufficient husks around it, remove them completely. Smear the corn with the butter and wrap each one with a sheet of tin foil. Barbecue as for recipe above.

Tying the pork shoulder with string, once the spice mixture has been rubbed into the meat, will keep it in shape and prevent any drying out during cooking.

Pulled Pork Barbecue
with hot pepper vinegar sauce

Gas	Indirect/Medium heat	✽ ✽
Charcoal	Indirect	
Prep time	5 minutes	
Grilling time	2 –3 hours	Serves 8

2 tablespoons paprika

1 tablespoon light soft brown sugar

1 tablespoon chilli powder

1 tablespoon ground cumin

1 tablespoon caster sugar

1½ teaspoons coarsely ground black pepper

2 teaspoons salt

2kg/4½lb boneless pork shoulder

Hot pepper vinegar sauce

175ml/6fl oz cider vinegar

175ml/6fl oz white wine vinegar

2 tablespoons caster sugar

½ teaspoon chilli flakes

½–1 teaspoon Tabasco

Salt and freshly ground black pepper

16 hamburger buns or crusty rolls

Coleslaw, to serve (optional)

1 Put the paprika, soft brown sugar, chilli powder, cumin, caster sugar, black pepper and salt into a small bowl and mix well. Rub the mixture all over the pork shoulder, pressing it well into the surface. Re-roll the pork and tie tightly with string at regular intervals around the meat.

2 Place the pork on the cooking grate and barbecue over Indirect Medium heat for 2½–3 hours, turning regularly, until very tender. Remove meat from the grill, cover and allow to rest for 10 minutes.

3 Meanwhile, prepare the **hot pepper vinegar sauce**: put the cider and wine vinegars, caster sugar, chilli flakes and Tabasco into a saucepan. Bring to the boil, simmer for 10 minutes until reduced by about one third, season to taste and put aside, but keep warm.

4 Shred, chop or pull the pork into pieces using two forks. In a bowl, mix the shredded pork well with the hot pepper vinegar sauce. Serve the pork in the buns or rolls with coleslaw (if using).

Kansas-City Spare Ribs
with tangy bbq rub

Gas	Indirect/Medium heat	✳ ✳	
Charcoal	Indirect		
Prep time	5 minutes + 2 hours marinating		Serves 6
Grilling time	1–1½ hours		

Tangy bbq rub
3 tablespoons sea salt
2 tablespoons paprika
1 tablespoon ground cumin
1 tablespoon dried oregano
2 teaspoons onion salt
1 teaspoon garlic granules
1 teaspoon freshly ground black pepper
½ teaspoon ground allspice
½ teaspoon ground cinnamon

1.5kg/3–3½lb pork back ribs, in one piece
1 quantity Weber® barbecue sauce (see page 140)

1 For the **tangy bbq rub**, put the salt, paprika, cumin, oregano, onion salt, garlic granules, black pepper, allspice and cinnamon into a small bowl and mix well. Spread all over the ribs, rubbing well into the meat. Put into a large non-metallic dish and chill for 2 hours.

2 Meanwhile, prepare the **Weber® barbecue sauce**, as the recipe shows on page 140. Set aside and reheat before serving.

3 Barbecue the ribs over Indirect Medium heat for 1–1½ hours, turning occasionally and brushing with the marinade during the last 20 minutes of grilling time. Allow to sit for 5 minutes before cutting the ribs into portions and serve with the warmed Weber® barbecue sauce.

Steak Tortilla Wraps
with Mexican side dips

Gas	Direct/Medium heat	✳ ✳	
Charcoal	Direct		
Prep time	20 minutes + 3–4 hrs marinating		Serves 6
Grilling time	10–19 minutes		

175ml/6fl oz lime juice (about 6 limes)
150ml/¼ pint vegetable juice
½ onion, finely chopped
1 tablespoon fresh parsley, chopped
2 garlic cloves, finely chopped
Salt and freshly ground black pepper
675g/1½lb rump tip or rump steak
2 red peppers, deseeded and thinly sliced
1 large onion, thinly sliced
1 tablespoon olive oil
Twelve 20cm/8 inch flour tortillas
Tomato salsa, to serve
Guacamole, to serve

1 Put the lime juice, vegetable juice, onion, parsley and garlic into a bowl and mix well. Put the steak into a non–metallic dish and pour over the marinade. Chill for 3–4 hours, turning the meat occasionally.

2 Meanwhile, cut a 45cm/18 inch square piece of heavy tin foil. Place the peppers and onion in the centre of the foil. Drizzle with the olive oil and season well. Bring the edges of the foil together and seal in the vegetables, to form a loose parcel.

3 Remove the steak from the marinade, reserving the marinade. Barbecue the meat over Direct Medium heat, 10–15 minutes for rare or 15–19 minutes for medium rare, turning once. Brush with the reserved marinade halfway through cooking time. Place the vegetable parcels on the cooking grate and cook for 12–14 minutes or until just tender.

4 Remove steak from grill and allow to rest for five minutes before slicing thinly. Meanwhile, wrap tortillas in tin foil. Place on the cooking grate for 5 minutes, turning once to heat through.

5 Serve the sliced meat in tortillas with peppers, onions, salsa and guacamole on the side.

Right: **Steak tortilla wrap.**

Rump tip or rump steak is perfect for cooking rare or medium rare. Avoid cooking too well done, as it will render the meat a little tough.

Let your guests fill and make up their own tortillas at the table.

vegetables
& vegetarian

For a long time the barbecue had been the domain of the carnivore with the occasional piece of fish or a stray corn on the cob making an appearance. Today vegetables and vegetarian food are in demand by everyone – vegetables have become an essential part of our diet and grilling is a great way to prepare them. Most vegetables can be grilled in no time, provide a kaleidoscope of colour, and offer good flavours and texture whether served alone or accompanied by grilled meats or fish. Vegetarian dishes are surprisingly quick to prepare and simple to cook. Delicious recipes range from goat's cheese and couscous filled peppers to chickpea burgers with tarragon mayonnaise, crispy onions to char grilled asparagus. Or, try the margarita pizza, which can be topped with an endless choice of vegetables.

perfect vegetables

Most vegetables can be grilled on the barbecue with few exceptions. Larger vegetables such as red and green peppers or onions can be grilled as they come, placed directly on the cooking grate and then turned with tongs. Smaller cuts of vegetables, or indeed small vegetables like mushrooms, are best skewered to make turning easier and quicker. Vegetables should be lightly brushed with olive oil before grilling to prevent them from sticking to the cooking grate. If you are grilling vegetables alongside marinated meats or fish, consider brushing the vegetables with the same marinade. Unless otherwise specified, all vegetables should be turned once halfway through grilling time. Experience will help you to know whether to put meats and vegetables on together, or one before the other.

Vegetables suitable for grilling

Times below are for crisp-tender vegetables. If you prefer more tender vegetables, allow longer grilling time.

■ **Asparagus** Bend the spears until they snap and discard the tough ends. Roll generously in olive oil, add Kosher salt and grill over Direct Medium heat for 5–6 minutes, turning occasionally, until marked by the grill and just tender.

■ **Aubergines** Trim the ends, then cut into thick slices width-ways or lengthways or into thick wedges. Cut baby aubergines in half. Oil and season very well, then grill over Direct Medium heat for 10–15 minutes.

■ **Corn on the cob** Smear the corn with butter and fold the husks back around the corn. Tie with cotton thread around the top to enclose. Arrange the corn on the cooking grate and grill over Indirect Medium heat for 20–30 minutes, until tender. (See page 110 for more ideas on grilling corn.)

■ **Courgettes** Trim ends and cut in half lengthways. If they are very large you can cut in three lengthways. Oil and season well and grill Directly over Medium heat for 8–15 minutes.

■ **Fennel** Cut off woody stems and cut into four or five thick slices. Brush with oil, season and grill over Direct Medium heat for 12–15 minutes until tender.

■ **Garlic** Garlic cloves can be skewered as part of a kebab, or cut a bulb in half and grill over Direct Medium heat for 8–10 minutes until softened. Whole garlic can also be roasted whole in aluminium foil parcels. Grill over Indirect Medium heat for 45–50 minutes, or until the garlic is very soft.

■ **Leeks** Use small or medium sized leeks. (Large winter leeks are unsuitable.) Cut off root ends and trim the green tops as usual, peel off the tough outer layer and cut in half lengthways. Wash well and pat dry on kitchen paper. Grill over Direct Medium heat for 12–15 minutes until tender, turning once.Grill whole leeks over Direct Medium heat for 14-16 minutes.

■ **Mushrooms** Cut and discard stems. Oil and season well and grill over Direct Medium heat for 8–10 minutes, until tender (depending on size). Skewer small mushrooms to make handling easier.

■ **Onions** Cut unpeeled onions in half and brush cut sides with oil. Grill over Direct High heat for 10–12 minutes, cut side down. Partially close vents in a charcoal grill to reduce heat; on a gas grill, turn to Low; grill for a further 35–40 minutes until richly caramelised. (Note, whole onions can also be peeled and roasted. Prepare in the same way as whole garlic.)

■ **Peppers** Cut into halves or quarters, discarding the seeds. Brush with oil and grill over Direct Medium heat for 6–8 minutes, turning once depending on the size. To roast whole peppers, brush each lightly with olive oil and roast over Indirect Medium heat for 15–20 minutes, until the outside is blackened and the pepper shape has collapsed. Allow to cool, then rub off the charred skin before cutting into portions, according to the recipe.

■ **Potatoes** Small or new potatoes can be cooked first in boiling water until just tender, then oiled and grilled over Direct heat until crisp. Larger potatoes, sweet potatoes or yams can be sliced thickly and brushed with oil and grilled for 10–12 minutes over Direct Medium heat. Whole large potatoes can be wrapped in foil and grilled over Indirect Medium heat for 50 minutes–1 hour for delicious baked potatoes.

■ **Radicchio** This robust salad leaf copes with the heat of a grill well. Cut into four wedges, brush the cut surfaces with oil and grill over Indirect Medium heat for 6–8 minutes.

■ **Squashes (patty pan and acorn)** Leave small squashes whole and cut larger ones in half lengthways. Brush with oil and grill over Direct Medium heat for 10–15 minutes.

■ **Tomatoes** Cut in half and grill over Direct Medium heat, cut side up, for 6–8 minutes until seared.

Vegetable kebabs

Many different vegetables can be skewered and cooked on the barbecue. Different vegetables will take different amounts of time to cook through. For example, peppers add good colour and flavour to kebabs and take about the same amount of time to cook as meat or poultry when cut to a similar size.

Vegetables most suitable for kebabs

■ Button mushrooms, left whole ■ Peppers, cut into bite size pieces ■ Onions, cut into wedges ■ Courgettes, cut into thick slices ■ New potatoes, pre-cooked ■ Small or baby leeks, cut into lengths ■ Baby aubergines, cut in half ■ Small artichokes, pre-cooked and cut in half ■ Patty pans and baby squashes ■ Cherry tomatoes, skewered on their own and cooked briefly.

Make sure to brush the kebabs well with oil, as mushrooms are very absorbent and will soak up a lot of the oil.

Halloumi Kebabs
with mushrooms & spicy peanut sauce

Gas	Indirect/Medium heat	❋ ❋
Charcoal	Indirect	
Prep time	45 minutes	
Grilling time	10 minutes	Serves 4

12 baby new potatoes
2 garlic cloves
375g/12oz Halloumi cheese
8 chestnut mushrooms
8 bay leaves
Oil, for brushing
Salt and freshly ground black pepper

Spicy peanut sauce
115g/4oz crunchy peanut butter
3 tablespoons sesame oil
1 red chilli, deseeded and chopped
1 garlic clove, crushed
1 tablespoon sweet chilli sauce
6 tablespoons warm vegetable stock
2 teaspoons soft light brown sugar
2 teaspoons dark soy sauce
1 tablespoon lemon juice

1 Put the potatoes into a saucepan of water, bring to the boil and cook for 15–20 minutes until tender. Drain and leave to cool completely.

2 Cut the two garlic cloves into thin slivers. With the tip of a sharp knife make incisions into the potatoes and insert a few slivers of garlic into each potato.

3 Cut the Halloumi cheese into twelve even sized pieces. Skewer the garlic potatoes, cheese, mushrooms and bay leaves onto 4 skewers. Brush with oil and season well. Put aside.

4 For the **spicy peanut sauce**, melt the peanut butter in a bowl, sitting over a saucepan of simmering water. Heat the sesame oil in a small saucepan, add the chilli and cook for 1 minute to soften. Beat into the warm peanut butter with the garlic, chilli sauce, vegetable stock, sugar, soy sauce and lemon juice and heat through. Keep warm.

5 Barbecue the kebabs over Indirect Medium heat for 10 minutes, turning once until vegetables are tender and cheese is golden. Divide the kebabs between 4 plates and drizzle with the warm spicy peanut sauce.

Chargrilled Asparagus Salad
with fresh Parmesan

Gas	Direct/Medium heat	✳
Charcoal	Direct	
Prep time	15 minutes	
Grilling time	5-6 minutes	Serves 4

24 asparagus spears

Oil, for brushing

3 tablespoons olive oil

2 tablespoons balsamic vinegar

Salt and freshly ground black pepper

175g/6oz rocket leaves

A large handful fresh basil leaves

75g/3oz Parmesan cheese

1 Trim the woody ends from the asparagus spears. Brush the asparagus with oil and lay the asparagus on the cooking grate, grilling over Direct Medium heat for 5-6 minutes, turning once, until marked by the grill. Leave aside to cool, then slice into pieces.

2 Whisk the olive oil, balsamic vinegar and seasoning. Toss with the rocket, basil leaves and asparagus spears.

3 Just before serving the salad drizzle balsamic dressing over and top with shavings of Parmesan cheese.

Chick Pea Burgers
with mayonnaise & crispy onions

Gas	Direct/Medium heat	✳ ✳
Charcoal	Direct	
Prep time	30 minutes plus chilling	
Grilling time	12 minutes	Serves 4

400g/14oz can chick peas, drained and rinsed

115g/4oz pine nuts

5 tablespoon olive oil

1 small onion, finely chopped

1 garlic clove, crushed

1 carrot, grated

2 tablespoons chopped fresh parsley

1 tablespoon tomato purée

1 tablespoon wholegrain mustard

1 egg, beaten

Salt and freshly ground black pepper

50g/2oz dried wholemeal breadcrumbs

2 small onions, finely sliced

1 tablespoon chopped fresh tarragon

4 tablespoons mayonnaise

1 Put the chickpeas into a large bowl and roughly mash with a fork. Dry fry the pine nuts in a frying pan until lightly golden all over and add to the chickpeas. Leave aside

2 Heat 1 tablespoon of the oil in a frying pan, add the chopped onion and garlic and sauté for 2–3 minutes until softened. Add this to the chickpeas and pine nuts then mix in the grated carrot, parsley, tomato purée, mustard, beaten egg and seasoning. Continue to mix until it comes together.

3 Divide the mixture and shape into four burgers. Put the bread-crumbs on a plate and use to coat the burgers evenly all over then chill for at least 1 hour to firm up.

4 Meanwhile heat the remaining oil in a small frying pan and cook the sliced onions for 8–10 minutes until deep golden and crisp. Drain well on kitchen paper and put aside.

5 Brush the burgers lightly on all sides with oil. Barbecue the burgers over Direct Medium heat for 10–12 minutes until golden, turning once. Meanwhile, stir the tarragon into the mayonnaise. Serve each burger on a plate, topped with a dollop of tarragon mayonnaise and sprinkled with crispy onions.

Left: **Chargrilled asparagus salad.**

Roasted Peppers
with goat cheese & couscous

Gas	Direct/Medium heat	☀
Charcoal	Direct	
Prep time	35 minutes	
Grilling time	10 minutes	Serves 4

100g/4oz quick cook couscous
300ml/½ pint hot vegetable stock
25g/1oz butter
1 tablespoon chopped fresh parsley
2 garlic cloves, crushed
16 black olives, roughly chopped
Salt and freshly ground black pepper
4 large red peppers
4 small tomatoes
225g/8oz goat cheese
Olive oil, for brushing

1 Put the couscous into a bowl and pour over the hot vegetable stock. Leave to soak for five minutes until the stock is absorbed and the couscous has softened. Add the butter, parsley, garlic, olives and seasoning and stir through with a fork.

2 Cut the peppers in half and remove and discard the seeds and white membrane. Cut the tomatoes in half and put a tomato half into each pepper half. Spoon the couscous mixture around the tomatoes.

3 Cut the goat's cheese into eight slices and put a slice in the middle of each pepper.

4 Brush the outside of the peppers with olive oil. Barbecue over Direct Medium heat for 8–10 minutes until peppers are just tender and slightly scorched. Serve with salad.

Rustic Sandwich
filled with grilled vegetables

Gas	Direct/Medium heat	☀
Charcoal	Direct	
Prep time	10 minutes	
Grilling time	13 minutes	Serves 4

2 red peppers, halved, deseeded and quartered
4 medium sized flat mushrooms
1 aubergine, cut into 1cm/½inch slices
50ml/2fl oz olive oil
Salt and freshly ground black pepper
2 tablespoons balsamic vinegar
115g/4oz mascarpone cheese
4 fresh ciabatta or other rustic bread rolls
Fresh basil sprigs, to serve

1 Brush the pepper quarters, mushrooms and aubergine slices with the olive oil. Barbecue the peppers over Direct Medium heat for 2–3 minutes.

2 Place the mushrooms and aubergine on the grill with the peppers and continue grilling for 8–10 minutes, turning occasionally, until all the vegetables are tender.

3 Put the vegetables into a large bowl, season and drizzle with the balsamic vinegar. Leave aside.

4 Split the rolls and toast each side on the grill. Spread the bottom half of each roll with the mascarpone cheese and top with the warm grilled vegetables and sprigs of basil. Replace the top of the bun and serve warm.

Above Left: **Rustic sandwich.**

Above Right: **Roasted peppers.**

Don't be afraid to let the skin on the peppers become quite blackened – this really adds to the flavour.

Beef tomatoes can vary in size, so if you have a little stuffing left over, fill another two or three tomatoes.

Stuffed Tomatoes
with salsa verde

Gas	Indirect/Medium heat	✹ ✹
Charcoal	Indirect	
Prep time	35 minutes	
Grilling time	8–10 minutes	Serves 6

400g/14oz can cannellini beans, drained and rinsed
1 tablespoon sun-dried tomato paste
Dash of Tabasco
50g/2oz fresh breadcrumbs
275g/10oz field mushrooms
2 tablespoons olive oil
1 onion, finely chopped
Salt and freshly ground black pepper
3 tablespoons chopped fresh parsley
12 large tomatoes
Oil, for brushing

Salsa verde
3 tablespoons chopped fresh parsley
1 tablespoon chopped fresh mint
3 tablespoons capers
1 garlic clove, crushed
1 tablespoon Dijon mustard
½ lemon, juice only
120ml/4fl oz extra virgin olive oil

1 Put the canellini beans into a bowl and roughly mash to break up slightly. Add the tomato paste, Tabasco and fresh bread-crumbs and mix well.

2 Cut the mushrooms into pieces and put into a food processor. Blend until finely chopped and almost paste like. Heat the olive oil in a large frying pan and fry the onion for 6–7 minutes until very soft. Stir in the mushrooms and cook for a further 10 minutes, stirring occasionally until all the liquid has evaporated. Stir into the bean mixture and season. Stir in the parsley and put aside.

3 Cut the top quarter off the tomatoes and put aside. Scoop out the tomato pulp and discard. Season the empty tomatoes. Spoon the bean and mushroom mixture into each. Replace tops.

4 Brush each tomato with a little oil and barbecue over Indirect Medium heat for 8–10 minutes until softened and the filling is hot.

5 Meanwhile, put all the ingredients for the **salsa verde** into a food processor and blend quickly to make a thick paste with a coarse texture. Season well and serve with the hot tomatoes.

Classic Pizza
margarita-style

Gas	Direct/Medium heat	
Charcoal	Direct	✳ ✳
Prep time	40 minutes + resting	
Grilling time	8 minutes	Serves 4

Pizza dough

2 teaspoons easy blend dried yeast

1 teaspoon sugar

350g/12oz plain flour

1 teaspoon salt

200ml/7fl oz warm water

1–2 tablespoons olive oil

Topping

2 tablespoons olive oil

1 small onion, finely chopped

1 garlic clove, crushed

½ teaspoon dried oregano

600g/21oz can chopped plum tomatoes

2 teaspoons caster sugar

Olive oil, for brushing

225g/8oz buffalo mozzarella, sliced and patted dry with kitchen paper

Large bunch basil leaves

1 For the **pizza dough** mix the yeast, sugar, flour and salt in a large bowl. Make a well in the centre, add the warm water and olive oil and mix well into a dough. Knead the dough lightly on a floured surface until smooth. Put into a clean bowl, cover and leave to rise in a warm place until doubled in size.

2 Meanwhile, to make the **topping**, heat the oil in a saucepan, sauté the onion and garlic for 2–3 minutes until softened, then add the oregano and tomatoes and cover and simmer for 10 minutes. Remove lid, add sugar and seasoning and cook uncovered for a further 10 minutes until the sauce is thickened.

3 Knead the dough again for a few minutes. Divide the dough in two and roll each piece into a circle, 25cm/10 inch in diameter. Brush one side of each base with olive oil and slide the bases onto two baking trays.

As the heat source is under the pizza, the mozzarella melts beautifully but does not go brown.

4 Using long-handled tongs, slide the bases, oil side down, onto the cooking grate and barbecue over Direct Medium heat for 2–3 minutes until the grill marks are visible. Slide back onto the baking sheet with the grilled side facing up.

5 Divide the tomato sauce between each crust and spread evenly with the back of a spoon, arranging the sliced mozzarella on top. Brush the cooking grate with oil and slide the pizzas back onto the cooking grate and barbecue for 3–4 minutes, until cheese is melted.

6 Remove from the heat and top each pizza with a handful of basil leaves. Serve half a pizza per person.

Cook's note

If you are short on time, use a convenient pizza dough mix and make up according to packet instructions.

salads, sauces & relishes

Complete the presentation of perfect barbecued food with a selection of flavourful salads and tasty relishes. A bowl of fresh tossed salad is the perfect complement to grilled meat, poultry and fish. Try potato, dill and caper salad with a juicy steak or a mixed leaf and summer herb salad with grilled fish. To avoid limp leaves, make the dressing and put it in the bottom of the salad bowl first, then pile the salad and vegetables on top. The salad can then be tossed together when ready to eat.

Forget old-fashioned labour intensive relishes and chutneys – the recipes in this chapter are easy and packed with flavour. Top your favourite food with green chilli sauce or traditional barbecue sauce, or for a fresh approach, try the tangy horseradish & beetroot relish. These and other delicious sides and salads add the finishing touch to barbecued food.

side salads

While it is tempting to think there is already a wealth of main meals to choose from and prepare, often the simplest side salad provides the crowning element to a meal. Salads are the perfect accompaniment across a range of fish, poultry and meat dishes, as they offer complementary flavours, refreshing colour and a contrasting 'bite' to the grilled food. It's quick and easy to provide a spread of individual side dishes that naturally support the main dish.

Barbecues are the perfect opportunity to take advantage of the freshest ingredients available in season, and as a rule, salad is the one dish that takes the least preparation.

Equally, the secret to sauces and relishes is that they blend a myriad of flavours within a meal; whether the flavour is fruity, tangy, spicy or creamy – they all have a place on the table.

Potato, Dill & Caper Salad

1.5 kg/3–3½lb large waxy potatoes
1 small red onion, chopped
4 tablespoons drained capers, chopped
4 tablespoons fresh dill, chopped
4 tablespoons soured cream
4 tablespoons mayonnaise
Salt and freshly ground black pepper

1 Wash the potatoes and cut into bite-size pieces. Boil in salted water for 10–12 minutes until tender, drain well and leave to cool. Put into a large bowl and add the capers and dill.

2 Mix the soured cream into the mayonnaise and pour over the potatoes. Toss gently together until well combined and season.

All salads will serve 6 ✳

Feta Cheese Salad
with broad, haricot & French beans

350g/12oz fresh or frozen broad beans
350g/12oz French beans, trimmed and halved
400g/14oz can haricot beans, drained and rinsed
115g/4oz feta cheese, diced
2 garlic cloves, finely chopped
1 shallot, finely chopped
2 tablespoons fresh parsley, chopped
4 tablespoons olive oil
1 tablespoon lemon juice
Salt and freshly ground black pepper

1 Cook the broad beans in boiling salted water for 1–2 minutes until just tender. Drain and refresh under cold running water then drain again and put into a large bowl.

2 Boil the French beans in salted water for 3 minutes until just tender. Drain and refresh under cold running water then drain again and add to the broad beans.

3 Add the haricot beans, feta, garlic, shallot and parsley. Whisk the oil and lemon juice together and pour over the bean mixture. Toss together and season to taste.

Above Left: **Feta cheese salad.**

Above Right: **Potato, dill and caper salad.**

Take advantage of food in season, when it is at its best and cheapest.

Peppers, onions and tomatoes represent the core flavours of the Mediterranean.

Mediterranean Salad
with grilled peppers & croutons

Gas	Direct/Medium heat	✳
Charcoal	Direct	
Prep time	20 minutes	
Grilling time	15 minutes	Serves 6

Oil for brushing
2 red peppers
2 green peppers
1 large bunch spring onions, trimmed
1 small loaf white bread
8 tablespoons olive oil
20 black olives
675g/1lb tomatoes
12 anchovy fillets drained and chopped
75g/3oz baby spinach leaves
2 garlic cloves, crushed
1 tablespoon Dijon mustard
2 tablespoons white wine vinegar
Salt and freshly ground black pepper

1 Brush the cooking grate with oil. Barbecue the red and green peppers over Direct Medium heat for 10–15 minutes, turning occasionally, until blackened and charred. Add the spring onions and barbecue for a further 4–5 minutes, turning once.

2 Put the hot peppers into a large bowl and cover with cling film and leave until cold. Cut the onions into lengths and put into a large bowl. When the peppers are cold remove the skins and seeds cut the peppers into strips and add to the spring onions.

3 Remove the crusts from the loaf of bread and cut the white bread into neat cubes about 2cm/¾ inch. Heat 4 tablespoons oil in a large frying pan and add the cubed bread and cook for 5–6 minutes tossing occasionally until golden all over. Drain on kitchen paper and cool.

4 Cut the tomatoes into wedges and put into the bowl with the pepper strips and onions. Add the anchovy fillets and spinach leaves and toss well.

5 Whisk the garlic, Dijon mustard, vinegar, seasoning and the remaining olive oil together. Drizzle the dressing over the salad. Scatter with the croutons.

Spiced Couscous Salad
with pine nuts & raisins

50g/2oz pine nuts
25g/1oz butter
¾ teaspoon ground cumin
¾ teaspoon ground cinnamon
¾ teaspoon ground coriander
¾ teaspoon ground allspice
2 teaspoons brown sugar
450ml/1 pint vegetable stock
350g/12oz couscous
115g/4oz raisins
3 tablespoons fresh coriander, chopped

1 Dry fry the pine nuts in a non-stick frying pan for 1–2 minutes until just golden. Put aside.

2 Melt the butter in a small saucepan and add the cumin, cinnamon, coriander, allspice and brown sugar and cook over a gentle heat for 1–2 minutes. Add the vegetable stock and bring to the boil. Stir in the couscous, cover and remove from the heat. Let it rest for 5 minutes until couscous is swelled and softened.

3 Using a fork stir through the reserved pine nuts, raisins, chopped coriander and seasoning.

Tomato Salad
with basil & mozzarella

350g/12oz baby plum tomatoes
350g/12oz cherry tomatoes
450g/12oz baby buffalo mozzarella, thickly sliced
25g/1oz basil leaves
1 tablespoon balsamic vinegar
2 tablespoons extra virgin olive oil
Salt and freshly ground black pepper

1 Cut 175g/6oz baby plum and 175g/6 oz cherry tomatoes in half and leave the remainder whole. Put into a large serving dish, add the mozzarella and basil leaves and mix well.

2 Whisk together the balsamic vinegar, olive oil and seasoning. Drizzle over the tomato and mozzarella.

Waldorf Salad

6 red dessert apples
6 celery sticks
75g/3oz walnut pieces
240ml/8fl oz mayonnaise
2 tablespoons lemon juice
Salt and freshly ground black pepper
2 heads of chicory (endive)
2 heads of Little Gem lettuce

1 Core the apples, cut into chunky dice and put into a large bowl. Thickly slice the celery and add to the apples. Add the walnut pieces.

2 Mix the mayonnaise with the lemon juice and seasoning until smooth. Add the dressing to the apple and celery mixture and toss together well.

3 Separate the chicory and little gem heads of lettuce into leaves. Break the leaves in half and toss together in a large bowl. Spoon the apple, celery and mayonnaise salad on top and garnish with celery leaves.

Mixed Leaf Salad
with summer herbs

75g/3oz baby spinach leaves
75g/3oz rocket leaves
75g/3oz lamb's lettuce
25g/1oz basil
25g/1oz chervil
25g/1oz chives
25g/1oz flat leaf parsley
1 small garlic clove, crushed
2 tablespoons lemon juice
4 tablespoons extra virgin olive oil
Salt and freshly ground black pepper

1 Put all the salad leaves and herbs into a large bowl and toss together well.

2 In a small bowl whisk together the garlic, lemon juice, olive oil and plenty of seasoning. Drizzle the dressing over the salad just before serving.

Right: **Waldorf salad.**

Left: **Spiced couscous salad.**

sauces & relishes

Fresh Hot Tomato Relish

450g/1lb plum tomatoes
2 tablespoons olive oil
1 shallot, finely chopped
2 garlic cloves, finely chopped
1 teaspoon dried chilli flakes
½ tablespoon caster sugar
2 tablespoons chopped fresh coriander
Salt and freshly ground black pepper

1 Using the tip of a sharp knife cut out the eye of each tomato and make a cross in the skin at the opposite end. Plunge into a large pan of boiling water for about 30 seconds. Quickly remove from the pan and plunge into cold water to arrest cooking. Peel away the skins.

2 Cut the tomatoes in half and scoop out the seeds and discard. Cut the tomato flesh into small neat dice and put aside.

3 Heat the oil in a saucepan and add the shallot and garlic and fry for 1–2 minutes. Add the chilli and cook for a further 1 minute then reduce to a gentle heat and cook for 5–6 minutes until very soft and colourless. Add the tomatoes and caster sugar and cook for 1–2 minutes. Remove from the heat and leave to cool. Stir in the chopped coriander, season and serve cold with steaks, sausages, chicken or fish.

Asian Sauce

120ml/4fl oz hoisin sauce
120 ml/4fl oz soy sauce
½ teaspoon sesame oil

In a small saucepan, combine all ingredients. Bring to the boil and immediately remove from the heat. Serve with grilled duck, chicken, beef or pork or brush onto meats during the last 10 minutes of cooking time. The sauce can keep in the refrigerator, covered, for up to 2 weeks.

Opposite Top: **Grated horseradish and beetroot relish.**

Opposite Centre: **Green chilli sauce.**

Opposite Bottom: **Fresh hot tomato relish.**

Grated Horseradish & Beetroot Relish

175g/6oz cooked beetroot
175g/6oz fresh horseradish, grated
1 tablespoon white wine vinegar
1 teaspoon caster sugar
Salt and freshly ground black pepper

Chop the beetroot coarsely and put into a bowl with the grated horseradish, vinegar, caster sugar and seasoning. Mix together well and leave for at least 30 minutes to allow flavours to develop. Serve with beef and fish.

Green Chilli Sauce

1 large green chilli
1 garlic clove, roughly chopped
1 lime, juice only
15g/½oz fresh coriander, roughly chopped
50ml/2fl oz soured cream
50ml/2fl oz mayonnaise
Salt and freshly ground black pepper

1 Roast the chilli over Direct Medium heat for 3–4 minutes, turning once or twice, until charred. Leave to cool. Remove the stem and seeds and chop roughly.

2 Put the chilli into a food processor along with the garlic, lime juice and coriander. Blend until very finely chopped, add the soured cream, mayonnaise and seasoning and process again until smooth. Serve with barbecued pork or chicken.

Weber® Barbecue Sauce

3 stalks celery, chopped
3 tablespoons chopped onion
2 tablespoons butter
2 tablespoons ketchup
2 tablespoons lemon juice
2 tablespoons sugar
2 tablespoons vinegar
1 tablespoon Worcestershire sauce
1 tablespoon dry mustard
Freshly ground black pepper

In a saucepan cook the celery and onion in the butter until tender. Add the remaining ingredients. Bring to a boil; reduce heat. Cover and simmer for 15 minutes. Serve warm.

Hot & Sweet Fruit Sauce

200g/7oz can apricots in natural juice
200g/7oz can peaches in natural juice
3 tablespoons lime juice
2 tablespoons vegetable oil
1 onion, finely chopped
1 garlic clove, crushed
5cm/2 inch piece fresh ginger grated
1 red chilli, deseeded and chopped
50g/2oz soft brown sugar
2 tablespoons dark soy sauce
75ml/3fl oz white wine vinegar
2 tablespoons tomato purée

1 Drain the apricots and peaches reserving the juice. Put the fruit, 3 tablespoons of the reserved juice and the lime juice into a food processor and blend to a smooth purée. Leave aside.
2 Heat the oil in a large saucepan and cook the onion for 4–5 minutes until very soft. Add the garlic, ginger and chilli and continue cooking for 3–4 minutes until softened.

3 Pour the fruit purée into the saucepan then the sugar, soy sauce, vinegar, tomato purée and seasoning, stirring well. Cook for 20 minutes until reduced slightly and thickened. Leave to cool. Serve cold with chicken, lamb, pork, vegetables or shellfish.

Classic Barbecue Sauce

1 teaspoon salt
125g/4oz granulated sugar
125g/4oz light brown soft sugar
750ml/1¼ pints cups beef stock
120ml/4fl oz Dijon mustard
50ml/2fl oz white wine vinegar
30ml/1fl oz liquid smoke (optional)
120ml/4fl oz Worcestershire sauce
250ml/8fl oz tomato purée
½ teaspoon chilli flakes
1 tablespoon chilli powder

1 Combine all the ingredients in a heavy-based saucepan. Bring to the boil and simmer gently, uncovered, for 1½–2 hours until thickened. Stir frequently, adding a little water if it starts reducing.

2 Brush onto grilled meats during the last 10 minutes of grilling time. The sauce can also be served to garnish grilled meats.

desserts

Hot sunny days and cool balmy evenings are accompanied by the desire for sharp zingy seasonal berries, crisp sweet meringues and cool melting ice cream. Luckily, delicious grilled fare can include a host of tempting summer desserts from mini pavlovas with honeyed plums to seared strawberry sundaes. Grilling fruits brings out their best – the sugars rise to the surface and caramelise, giving off wonderful aromas and a special flavour that can be enjoyed alone or paired with cakes, ice-creams or sauces. Even baked desserts usually associated with indoors get a look in; try cherry and almond crumbles or pear and ginger puddings which can bake unattended, while host and guests enjoy the main course.

perfect fruit

Barbecued fruits are a wonderfully fresh way to finish a barbecue. Most soft fruits and some hard fruits such as apples and pears can be barbecued, but the most popular tend to be the tropical fruits such as pineapple, banana and mango. Whatever fruit you intend to use, always clean the cooking grate well after cooking savoury foods and brush it with a little oil (use one with virtually no flavour such as groundnut or sunflower). Fruits should only be grilled long enough to caramelise their natural sugars. Although peaches and apples can be barbecued to accompany meats and fish, most fruits are barbecued to serve for dessert and nothing tastes better than hot grilled fruits served over cold melting ice cream.

Fruit suitable for grilling

■ **Apples** Peel if you want to, although the skin helps them stay together if they overcook. Halve and remove cores and grill over Indirect Medium heat for 15–20 minutes, turning once. Whole apples can be barbecued over Indirect Medium heat for 35-40 minutes.

■ **Apricots** Cut in half; discard stones. Thread onto skewers and grill cut side down over Direct Medium heat for 6–8 minutes.

■ **Bananas** Halve lengthways, grill cut side down for grill marks, then grill skin side down over Direct Medium heat for 6–8 minutes.

■ **Figs** Using a small sharp knife, cut a cross in the figs about three quarters way through the fruit and open out like a flower. Grill over Direct Low heat for 8–10 minutes until the figs are soft.

■ **Mango** Cut in half and discard the stone and cut into thick slices. Grill over Direct Medium heat for 8–10 minutes.

■ **Nectarines** Cut in half lengthways, discarding stones and grill cut side down over Direct Medium heat for 8–10 minutes.

■ **Pawpaws** Peel if you want to. Cut lengthways into thick wedges, discarding black seeds. Grill cut side down over Direct Medium heat for 8–10 minutes.

■ **Peaches** Peel if you want to. Cut in half and grill cut side down over Direct Medium heat for 8–10 minutes.

■ **Pears** Peel if you want to. Cut into halves or quarters and remove core. Grill cut side down over Direct Medium heat for 10–14 minutes.

■ **Pineapple** Top and tail and cut off the thick skin. Dig out any tough eyes. Cut into slices and remove the core with a small cutter or knife. Grill over Direct Medium heat for 6–10 minutes; thread smaller pieces on a skewer. Turn once during grilling time.

■ **Strawberries** Grill whole over Indirect Medium heat for 4–5 minutes – threading on a skewer helps make turning the fruit easier.

Fruit kebabs

This is a fun way to serve a selection of fruit. Cut fruit into similar size pieces. Use wooden or bamboo skewers, as moist fruit spins around on smooth metal skewers. Soak the skewers in cold water first for at least 30 minutes. Brush the cooking grate with oil and barbecue kebabs over Direct Medium heat for 6–10 minutes, turning once. Brush kebabs with a mixture of liquid honey and lime juice halfway through grilling time.

Right: **Mixed fruit kebabs provide a tangy and colourful finale to an *al fresco* meal.**

The individual Pavlova nests will keep for 3–4 days if stored in an airtight container, making it even easier to plan the dessert in advance.

The honey glaze over the plums will not only sweeten them, but also help to soften the fruit during grilling.

Pavlova
with honey-seared plums

Gas	Indirect/Medium heat	☀ ☀
Charcoal	Indirect	
Prep time	2 hours	
Grilling time	5–6 minutes	Serves 6

4 egg whites
Pinch of salt
225g/8oz caster sugar
2 teaspoons cornflour
1 teaspoon white wine vinegar
250g/9oz mascarpone cheese
300ml/½pint double cream
2 tablespoons caster sugar
9 ripe plums
1 tablespoon liquid honey

1 Preheat the oven to 180°C/350°F/Gas 4. Lightly grease two large baking trays and line with non-stick greaseproof paper. Put aside.

2 In a clean bowl whisk the egg whites with the salt until soft peaks form. Gradually whisk in the caster sugar, a little at a time, to give a stiff glossy meringue mixture. Whisk in the cornflour and vinegar. Take a large spoonful of the meringue and spoon onto one of the lined baking trays and form into a round. Make a slight dent in the centre with the back of the spoon to give a nest shape. Repeat to make six in all, spaced well apart. Bake for 5 minutes then reduce oven temperature to 150°C/275°F/Gas 1 and bake for a further 1 hour 15 minutes. Leave to cool on the baking trays.

3 Meanwhile, in a clean bowl, whisk the mascarpone cheese until softened. In a separate bowl whisk half the double cream and caster sugar until soft peaks form. Fold into the softened mascarpone with the remaining cream until smooth. Cover and chill until required.

4 Soak six short bamboo skewers in cold water for at least 30 minutes. Cut the plums in half and remove stones. Thread three halves onto each skewer, cutting the skewer to size if necessary. Brush with the honey. Barbecue over Indirect Medium heat for 5-6 minutes until just softened.

5 Peel the meringues off the paper and spoon the mascarpone cream into each. Serve each meringue with a warm skewer of grilled plums.

Green-peppered Pineapple
with orange caramel

Gas	Direct/Medium heat	✳ ✳
Charcoal	Direct	
Prep time	5 minutes	
Grilling time	6–7 minutes	Serves 4

**1 teaspoon green peppercorns in brine, drained
and roughly chopped**
4 thick slices fresh pineapple
2 teaspoons caster sugar

Orange caramel
125 g/4 oz granulated sugar
1 orange, rind and juice
50ml/2fl oz single cream
Good quality vanilla ice cream, to serve

1 Rub the peppercorns into both sides of each pineapple slice. Sprinkle one side of each slice with the sugar.

2 Place pineapple slices, sugar side down, in the centre of the cooking grate. Barbecue over Direct Medium heat for 6–7 minutes or until browned.

3 Meanwhile, for the **orange caramel**, put the granulated sugar and orange rind into a small saucepan with 2 tablespoons cold water, and heat gently until dissolved. Bring to the boil and cook for 4–5 minutes until a golden caramel colour. Remove from the heat and stir in the orange juice and the cream then return to the heat and cook gently, stirring until smooth. Leave aside.

4 To serve, put the grilled pineapple slices into four serving dishes and pour over the warm orange caramel.

Grilled Figs
Spanish style

Gas	Direct/Low heat	✳ ✳
Charcoal	Direct	
Prep time	20 minutes	
Grilling time	6-8 minutes	Serves 6

1 vanilla bean
115g/4oz fresh, soft goat's cheese
300ml/½ pint double cream
2 tablespoons caster sugar
12 fresh figs
50g/2oz good quality plain chocolate

1 With the tip of a sharp knife split open the vanilla bean and scrape out the seeds. Put the seeds into a bowl with goat's cheese and beat well. In a clean bowl whip the double cream with the caster sugar to soft peaks then fold into the vanilla flavoured goat's cheese. Chill until required.

2 Using a small sharp knife, cut a cross in the figs about three quarters way through the fruit and open out like a flower.

3 Cut the chocolate into twelve small nuggets. Bury a nugget of chocolate in the centre of each fig, then barbecue the figs over Direct Low heat for 6–8 minutes until chocolate is melted and figs are soft.

4 Serve two hot figs per person on a serving plate with a scoop of the vanilla goat's cream.

The orange juice will be absorbed by the banana halves during grilling.

Sprinkle the surface of the banana halves evenly with the caramel mixture to avoid one side being overcooked.

Caramelised Bananas
with coconut & orange

Gas	Direct/High heat	☀
Charcoal	Direct	
Prep time	30 minutes	
Grilling time	5 minutes	Serves 6

Oil, for brushing
7 tablespoons caster sugar
2 tablespoons desiccated coconut
Grated rind of 1 orange, reserve fruit for the juice
300ml/½ pint double cream
2 tablespoons rum
6 large bananas

1 Brush a baking tray with a little oil and put aside. In a saucepan put 6 tablespoons of the caster sugar with 2 tablespoons cold water. Dissolve the sugar slowly, then bring to the boil and cook for 6–8 minutes until it turns a golden caramel colour. Remove from the heat and stir in the coconut and orange rind.

2 Pour caramel onto the oiled baking tray and put aside for 10 minutes to set. When set hard break into pieces and put into a food processor and grind to a powder. Put aside.

3 Meanwhile whip the cream with the remaining caster sugar and rum until soft peaks form. Chill until required.

4 Cut the bananas in half lengthways. Squeeze a little juice from the orange over the banana halves and then sprinkle the surface of each half with the caramel and coconut. Barbecue skin side down over Direct Medium heat for 5 minutes until the caramel mixture is melted and golden. Serve warm with the rum cream. Decorate with orange zest.

Cook's note

You can make the caramel and coconut powder in advance; however, make sure to keep it in an airtight container and use on the same day.

Peach Parcels
with Amaretti-filled centres

Gas	Indirect/High heat	
Charcoal	Indirect	✳
Prep time	20 minutes	
Grilling time	15 minutes	Serves 6

115g/4oz amaretti biscuits
75g/3oz flaked almonds
50g/2oz light muscovado sugar
75g/3oz butter, diced
1 lemon, grated rind and juice
1 large egg yolk, beaten
6 ripe peaches

1 Crush the amaretti biscuits roughly and put into a large bowl. Add the almonds, muscovado sugar, butter and lemon rind. Work the mixture with your fingertips until the mixture resembles coarse breadcrumbs. Add the egg yolk and mix well until mixture is just sticking together.

2 Cut the peaches in half then remove the stones and discard. Dip each peach half in lemon juice. Divide the filling amongst the peach halves, pressing down lightly to fill the cavity.

3 Take six large squares of extra thick tin foil about 20cm/8 inch square. Put two filled peach halves on each square and bring edges together and scrunch together to loosely seal in peaches. Barbecue over Indirect High heat for 15 minutes until the peaches are soft and the filling is sizzling. Serve hot with scoops of vanilla ice cream.

Kirsch-soaked Cherries
with almond crumble

Gas	Indirect/Medium heat	
Charcoal	Indirect	✳ ✳
Prep time	35 minutes	
Grilling time	20 minutes	Serves 6

675g/1½lb fresh cherries, or two 400g/14oz cans
    cherries in syrup
2 tablespoons Kirsch
1 orange, grated rind only

Crumble topping
200g/7oz plain flour
150g/5oz butter, diced
75g/3oz flaked almonds
150g/6oz brown sugar

Crème fraiche, for garnish

1 If using fresh cherries, stone the cherries first. Put into a large bowl and pour over the Kirsch. Add the orange rind and mix well. If using tinned cherries in syrup, drain very well and mix with the Kirsch and orange rind and put aside.

2 For the **crumble topping**, put the flour into a large bowl with the butter. Using your fingertips, rub in the butter until the mixture resembles rough breadcrumbs, then stir in the almonds and brown sugar.

3 Divide the cherries between six small heatproof dishes, or large ramekins, or place them in one large shallow pie dish. Top with the crumble mixture. Place on the cooking grate and barbecue over Indirect Medium heat for 20 minutes until the top is golden and the cherry mixture is bubbling. Leave to cool slightly before serving with spoonfuls of crème fraiche.

Above Left: **Peach parcels.**

Above Right: **Kirsch-soaked cherries with almond crumble.**

Fresh peaches are best for this dessert, although you can use drained tinned peaches. They will cook very soft, but are still delicious.

Sticky Pear
& ginger puddings

Gas	Indirect/Medium heat	✳ ✳	
Charcoal	Indirect		
Prep time	20 minutes		
Grilling time	18–20 minutes		Serves 4

Butter for greasing
Flour for dusting
1 ripe pear
75g/3oz butter
130g/4½oz light brown sugar
50g/2oz plain flour
¼ teaspoon baking soda
½ teaspoon ground ginger
½ teaspoon ground cinnamon
Large pinch nutmeg
50ml/2fl oz golden syrup
1 large egg, beaten

1 Brush four 17ml/6fl oz individual pudding moulds with a little butter. Dust each with flour and put aside.

2 Peel the pear and cut into quarters. Cut the core from each quarter and dice the pear finely. Divide between the four pudding moulds. Put 50g/2oz of the butter into a saucepan with the brown sugar and heat gently, stirring well until melted and well combined. Pour over the diced pear. Leave aside.

3 Sift the flour, baking soda, ground ginger, cinnamon and nutmeg together onto a sheet of greaseproof paper. Reserve.

4 Melt the remaining butter, remove from heat and beat in the golden syrup. Make sure it's cooled and then beat in the egg. Beat in the sieved dry ingredients.

4 Divide the mixture between the four moulds. Put the moulds on the cooking grate and barbecue over Indirect Medium heat for 18–20 minutes, until golden.

5 Let the puddings cool slightly, then turn out and serve warm with scoops of vanilla ice cream.

Cook's note

These puddings can be made in advance, covered with cling film and put aside. They can be cooked while you and your guests enjoy the main course.

Seared Strawberry
& vanilla sundae

Gas	Indirect /Medium heat	✳	
Charcoal	Indirect		
Prep time	20 minutes		
Grilling time	6 minutes		Serves 4

900g/2lb strawberries
4 tablespoons icing sugar
3 teaspoons balsamic vinegar
150ml/¼ pint double cream
3 tablespoons chopped nuts
Good quality vanilla ice cream, to serve

1 Put half the strawberries, 2 tablespoons of icing sugar and balsamic vinegar into a food processor or blender and blend to a smooth sauce. Chill until required.

2 Whip the double cream and 1 tablespoon icing sugar to stiff peaks and chill. Toast the nuts under a pre-heated grill until golden brown. Put aside to cool.

3 Thread the remaining strawberries onto two or three metal skewers (this makes them easier to turn) and dust with the remaining icing sugar. Barbecue over Indirect Medium heat for 6 minutes, turning once, until soft and marked with the grill.

4 Spoon a little sauce into the bottom of four sundae glasses and top with two scoops of vanilla ice cream. Take the grilled strawberries off the skewers and divide between the glasses, reserving four for decoration. Spoon the whipped cream on top. Pour over more strawberry sauce and decorate with chopped nuts and reserved strawberries.

Right: **Seared strawberry & vanilla sundae.**

index

acknowledgements

Weber and the editors wish to thank the following people for their valuable contribution to this book: Debby Nakos; Jeff Stephen; Edna Schlosser; Marsha Capen; Susan Radcliffe; Susan Maruyama; Gareth Jenkins; Sonia Cauvin and everyone at Perdiguier.